W9-CQX-798

GETTING BY IN
FRENCH

Second Edition

A QUICK BEGINNER'S COURSE FOR
TOURISTS AND BUSINESS PEOPLE

Pierrick Picot

BARRON'S

In cooperation with BBC Languages

First edition for the United States
published 1996 by Barron's Educational Series, Inc.
in cooperation with BBC Languages
a division of BBC Worldwide Ltd.
Woodlands, 80 Wood Lane, London W12 OTT

A Word to the Reader:

Because exchange rates of foreign currencies against the U.S. dollar vary from day to day, the actual cost of a hotel room, a taxi ride, or a meal may be more or less than the amounts in this book. Please consult a newspaper, bank, or currency house for the most up-to-date exchange rate.

© Copyright 1992 by Pierrick Picot

Portions of the Reference section of this book from *French at a Glance* by Gail Stein

All rights reserved.
No part of this book may be reproduced in any
form, by photostat, microfilm, xerography, or
any other means, or incorporated into any
information retrieval system, electronic or
mechanical, without the written permission of
the copyright owner.

All inquiries should be addressed to:
Barron's Educational Series, Inc.
250 Wireless Boulevard
Hauppauge, New York 11788

Library of Congress Catalog Card No. 95-52729
International Standard Book No. 0-8120-9678-9 (book)
                              0-8120-8440-3 (book/cassette package)

Library of Congress Cataloging-in-Publication Data
Picot, Pierrick.
    Getting by in French : a quick beginner's course for tourists and business people /
    Pierrick Picot.
        p.   cm. — (Get by in—)
    ISBN 0-8120-8440-3 (book-cassette pkg.). — ISBN 0-8120-9678-9 (book)
    1. French language—Conversation and phrase books.   I. Title.   II. Series.
PC2121.P613 1996
448.3'421—dc20   95-52729
                                                                   CIP

Printed in Hong Kong

987654

CONTENTS

INTRODUCTION

Barron's *Getting by in French* is a six-unit course for anyone planning a visit to a French-speaking country. It provides a basic "survival kit" for some of the situations you're likely to find yourself in.

Getting by in French is especially designed for those who have little or no knowledge of French, so that they can get more enjoyment out of their trips abroad. The course consists of two audio-cassettes and this book.

The *audiocassettes* concentrate on what you'll need to say and understand to cope with a particular situation—getting something to eat and drink, finding somewhere to stay, asking the way, for example. They include real-life conversations recorded in France, to let you hear everyday French right from the start. They also give you opportunities to repeat words and phrases you hear in the conversations and to work out for yourself how to "get by."

All the recordings were made during Marie-Pierre's visit to Angers in western France. Angers is situated on the river Maine, 90 minutes from Paris by TGV (train à grande vitesse), France's high-speed train. Gateway to the châteaux of the Loire Valley, Angers is an elegant and pleasant town to visit with its picturesque streets, gardens, and parks.

Each of the first six units of *Getting by in French* is made up of six parts:
- the key words and expressions you'll need to follow the recorded conversations.
- the texts of the recorded conversations.
- additional words and phrases you've come across in the conversations.
- some explanations of the language used.
- exercises, for you to practice what you've learned.

- some information you may find useful while in France.

At the back of the book, you'll find a useful Reference Section including, for example, a list of numbers, the key to the exercises, and a French-English vocabulary.

TO MAKE THE MOST OF THE COURSE

- Start by reading the key words and expressions.
- Listen carefully to the cassette, joining in the activities and exercises as you go along. It's best not to read the printed conversations the first time around so that you can see how much you can understand without them. Play the same conversation as many times as you like. Use the additional words and phrases if you need to.
- Then read the explanations.
- Finally, try out what you've been learning in the exercises. Keys are at the back of the book.

It's a good idea, if you can, to work through the exercises with someone else. You'll also have plenty of opportunities to practice your pronunciation using the cassette. At the end of Side B of Cassette 2 there is a recording of all the words in the Pronunciation Guide at the back of this book, with pauses for you to repeat them.

Good luck with your French . . . *Bonne chance!*

1 MEETING PEOPLE & ORDERING DRINKS

KEY WORDS AND PHRASES

bonjour	good morning, good afternoon
bonsoir	good evening, good night
au revoir	goodbye
Comment allez-vous?	How are you?
Ça va?	How are things?
Ça va!	Fine!
Vous êtes d'Angers?	Are you from Angers?
Vous êtes d'où?	Where are you from?
je suis de Lille	I'm from Lille
s'il vous plaît	please
merci	thank you
un thé, s'il vous plaît	a tea, please
deux bières, s'il vous plaît	two beers, please

CONVERSATIONS

HELLO, HOW ARE THINGS?

ANNE	Bonjour, Marie-Noël.
MARIE-NOEL	Bonjour, Anne.
ANNE	Ça va?
MARIE-NOEL	Ça va. Et vous?
ANNE	Très bien, merci.

GOOD MORNING, HOW ARE YOU?

M. DOREAU	Bonjour, Monsieur Bouillon. Comment allez-vous?
M. BOUILLON	Très bien, je vous remercie. Et vous-même?
M. DOREAU	Ça va très bien.

GOOD EVENING

BEATRICE	Oh, bonsoir.
PIERRICK	Bonsoir, Béatrice. Voici Marie-Pierre.
BEATRICE	Bonsoir, Marie-Pierre.
MARIE-PIERRE	Bonsoir, Béatrice.

GOODBYE, THANK YOU VERY MUCH

MARIE-PIERRE	Au revoir, madame, et merci beaucoup.
MME HOPPELER	Au revoir, madame.
PIERRICK	Au revoir, madame.
MME HOPPELER	Au revoir, monsieur.
PIERRICK	Merci.

ARE YOU FROM ANGERS?

MARIE-PIERRE	Béatrice, vous êtes d'Angers?
BEATRICE	Non, je suis de Lille.

WHERE ARE YOU FROM?

MARIE-PIERRE	Monsieur Michaud, vous êtes d'Angers?
M. MICHAUD	Non, je ne suis pas d'Angers.
MARIE-PIERRE	Vous êtes d'où alors?
M. MICHAUD	Je suis d'Avignon.

I'M ENGLISH

MARIE-PIERRE	Vous n'êtes pas française?
BARBARA	Non, non. Je suis anglaise.
MARIE-PIERRE	Ah, vous êtes anglaise! Et vous êtes d'où?
BARBARA	Je suis de Chichester.

BREAKFAST

SERVEUSE	Bonjour.
MARIE-PIERRE	Bonjour.
SERVEUSE	Vous désirez? Café, thé ou chocolat?
MARIE-PIERRE	Chocolat, s'il vous plaît.
SERVEUSE	D'accord. Je vous sers tout de suite.

AT THE *PATISSERIE*

MME GABORIEAU	Que désirez-vous, monsieur-dame?
PIERRICK	Deux thés, s'il vous plaît.
MME GABORIEAU	Oui. Nature, lait, citron?
MARIE-PIERRE	Un thé au lait, s'il vous plaît.
MME GABORIEAU	Oui. Et pour monsieur?
PIERRICK	Au citron, s'il vous plaît.
MME GABORIEAU	Oui.

ORDERING DRINKS

PIERRICK	S'il vous plaît.
M. MENARD	Bonsoir, messieurs-dame. Que désirez-vous boire?
PIERRICK	Marie-Pierre?
MARIE-PIERRE	Un citron pressé pour moi, s'il vous plaît.
PIERRICK	Et deux bières, s'il vous plaît.
M. MENARD	Deux bières? Bouteille ou pression?
PIERRICK	Pour vous Didier?
DIDIER	Bouteille, s'il vous plaît.
PIERRICK	Et pour moi pression.
M. MENARD	Bien sûr.

AN APERITIF?

BEATRICE	Vous voulez un apéritif?
PIERRICK	Oui, merci. Oui.
MARIE-PIERRE	Oui, merci.
BEATRICE	Du martini, du whisky, du porto, du jus d'orange?

MARIE-PIERRE	Pour moi un martini, s'il vous plaît.
BEATRICE	Et Pierrick?
PIERRICK	Et moi un whisky.
BEATRICE	D'accord.

CHEERS!

PIERRICK	Tchin, tchin!
MARIE-PIERRE	Tchin, tchin!
BEATRICE	Tchin!
PIERRICK	A la vôtre!
BEATRICE	A la vôtre!

NUMBERS

PIERRICK	Tu sais compter jusqu'à dix?
FABIEN	Oui.
PIERRICK	Vas-y.
FABIEN	Un, deux, trois, quatre, cinq, six, sept, huit, neuf, dix.
PIERRICK	Allez. Vas-y encore. Lentement.
FABIEN	Un, deux, trois, quatre, cinq, six, sept, huit, neuf, dix.
PIERRICK	Très bien!

WORD LIST

très bien	very well
je vous remercie	thank you
. . . et vous(-même)?	. . . and you(rself)?
Vous êtes d'Angers?	Are you from Angers?
Vous êtes d'où?	Where are you from?
je suis d'Avignon	I'm from Avignon
Vous désirez?	What would you like?
Désirez-vous . . . ?/	Would you like . . . ?
Vous voulez . . . ?	

d'accord	fine/right/OK
je vous sers tout de suite	I'll serve you right away
le thé nature	plain tea
le thé au lait	tea with milk
le thé citron	tea with lemon
Que désirez-vous boire?	What would you like to drink?
une bière	beer
Bouteille ou pression (f)?	Bottle or draft?
bien sûr	of course
un porto	port
un jus d'orange	orange juice
A la vôtre/Tchin!	Your health!/Cheers!
Tu sais compter . . . ?	Can you count . . . ?
jusqu'à	up to
vas-y	go on
lentement	slowly

EXPLANATIONS

GREETINGS AND GOODBYES

Bonjour means 'hello' during the day, but say *Bonsoir* in the evening.
Au revoir means 'goodbye' at any time, or you can say *Bonsoir* in the evening.

You can add *madame, mademoiselle* or *monsieur*:
Bonjour, monsieur
Au revoir, madame

If it's someone you know, you can add their name:
Bonjour, Monsieur Bouillon
Bonsoir, Béatrice

In a café or a restaurant, you may be greeted with: *Bonjour, monsieur-dame*, or if there are several of you: *Bonsoir, messieurs-dames*. Don't be surprised if it sounds more like: *'jour, 'sieurs-dames!*

HOW ARE YOU?

To ask how someone is, say:
Comment allez-vous?
Or if it's someone you know:
Ça va?
If someone asks you how you are, you can reply:

(Oui) bien,
(Oui) je vais bien,
(Oui) très bien,   *merci*
Ça va,

People may also ask: *Vous allez bien?* Or if you don't look
well: *Ça va pas?* If you're feeling under the weather, say: *Non,*
ça ne va pas or just *Non, ça va pas* which is 'No I'm not feeling
well'. You will often hear people leave out the *ne* in negative
sentences: *Je sais pas* (I don't know); *Je peux pas* (I can't).

PLEASE AND THANK YOU

S'il vous plaît is 'please'. You use it when you ask for
something, but also to attract the waiter's attention:
S'il vous plaît!
Oui? Que désirez-vous?

Merci accompanied by *beaucoup* or *bien,* is 'thank you' or
'thank you very much'. Be careful! *Merci* by itself can mean
'no thank you', if you want to decline an offer of food, for
example. To make your meaning clear, say: *Oui, merci* or *Non,*
merci. You can also say: *Je vous remercie.*

ORDERING DRINKS

The simplest way is to say what you want and add *s'il vous*
plaît.

Un thé au lait,
Deux bières,
Un citron pressé (freshly squeezed lemon juice)   *s'il vous plaît*

MASCULINE AND FEMININE

In French, both people and things are either masculine or feminine; it's best to learn which words are which as you go along.

With masculine words, you use *un*, which is 'a' or 'an': *un thé, un citron pressé, un apéritif, un pub*. With feminine nouns, you use *une* which is also 'a' or 'an': *une bière, une bouteille, une pression, une pâtisserie*.

NUMBERS

For numbers one to ten, say:
un   deux   trois   quatre   cinq   six   sept   huit   neuf   dix

Numbers are important for placing orders, dealing with prices, dates, times, hotel rooms, etc. If you don't understand them first time, ask for them to be repeated slowly: *Lentement, s'il vous plaît* or more slowly: *Plus lentement, s'il vous plaît*.

WHERE ARE YOU FROM?

To ask people where they're from, say, for example:
Vous êtes de Lille? Are you from Lille?
Vous êtes d'où? Where are you from?

To answer these questions, say:
Oui, je suis de Lille
Non, je suis d'Angers
Je suis de Chichester
If the word following *de* begins with a vowel, you shorten *de* to *d'*: *Vous êtes d'où? Je suis d'Angers*.

NATIONALITIES

To exchange information about nationalities, you can again use *Vous êtes . . . ?* and *Je suis . . .*:
Vous êtes français? (French)
Vous êtes anglais? (English)

Vous êtes américain? (American)

If you're asking a woman, you add an *-e:*
Vous êtes écossaise? (Scottish)
Vous êtes galloise? (Welsh)
Vous êtes irlandaise? (Irish)
To answer, say:
Oui, je suis écossais(e).
Non, je suis anglais(e).

EXERCISES

1 GREETINGS

a   Greet your friend Marie-Pierre and ask if she's OK.
b   You meet Anne in the evening. How do you greet her?
c   Say 'good morning' to Monsieur Bouillon and ask him
    how he is.
d   Say goodbye to Monsieur Doreau.
e   You've met a woman whose name you don't know.
    Greet her.

2 AT THE 'CAFE'

What is your side of this conversation?

VOUS	*Call the waiter.*
M. MENARD	Bonjour, monsieur-dame. Vous désirez?
VOUS	*Ask for two beers.*
M. MENARD	Bouteille ou pression?
VOUS	*Draft, please.*
M. MENARD	D'accord.

3 NUMBERS

a   Fill in the missing numbers:
    un   deux   . . .   quatre   . . .   six   . .   . .   neuf   . . .

b Work out the following:

six + quatre = . . .

deux + trois = . . .

un + cinq = . . .

sept + deux = . . .

huit + deux = . . .

4 ORDERING DRINKS

Have a look at the drink list, then tell the waiter what you
want:

BOISSONS

Thé nature	10,00 F
Thé citron	11,50 F
Café	6,00 F
Jus d'orange	11,00 F
Jus de tomate	11,00 F

ALCOOLS ET LIQUEURS

Cointreau	23,00 F
Cognac	23,00 F
Rhum	20,00 F

a A lemon tea, please.

b Two coffees, please.

c Three orange juices, please.

d One cointreau, please.

5 MIX AND MATCH

Match the questions and answers:

1 Vous êtes écossaise?   **a** Ça va très bien merci.

2 Et vous?   **b** Non, je suis d'Edimbourg.

3 Vous êtes de Glasgow?   **c** Non, je suis française.

4 Vous êtes galloise?   **d** Moi, je suis anglais.

5 Ça va?   **e** Oui, je suis de Cardiff.

WORTH KNOWING

GREETINGS AND GOODBYES

In France, greeting people is often accompanied by a handshake. If you know someone well, you're more likely to kiss each other on both cheeks – two, three or even four times, depending on local custom.

You can use *Bonjour* at any time during the day, except in the evening. It literally means 'good day' and it's used for both 'good morning' and 'good afternoon'. You may often hear *Bon après-midi*. This isn't a greeting but means 'Have a good afternoon'. Similarly, *Bonne soirée* me ins 'Have a good evening'.

If you're introduced to someone, you can reply *Enchanté* (Pleased to meet you) or *Bienvenu* (Welcome).

Bonsoir is used in the evening roughly after 6 p.m. You can use it both when you meet and when you leave people.

Au revoir can be used at any time to say goodbye.

People don't use first names as readily as in America, especially when they don't know you very well. If in doubt, wait for the other person to take the first step.

Young people tend to say *Salut!*, both when they meet and when they leave each other, accompanied by kisses on the cheeks or, between men, a handshake.

DRINKS

une eau minérale mineral water

un fruit pressé freshly squeezed fruit juice (*orange, citron . . .*)
(orange, lemon . . .)

un diabolo (menthe, fraise . . .) lemonade (with mint,
strawberry syrup)

un jus d'ananas pineapple juice

une limonade lemonade

un martini dry vermouth

une pression draft beer

une bière bouteille bottled beer

un panaché lager shandy (beer and ginger ale)

un café crème coffee with milk

un décafeiné decaffeinated coffee

un chocolat (chaud) (hot) chocolate

une infusion (menthe, tilleul) herbal tea (mint, lime)

un pastis / un ricard liqueur with aniseed

un porto blanc ou *rouge* white *or* red port

One of the ways to say 'Cheers' or 'Your health!' is *Tchin-
tchin!* Other expressions include *A votre santé! A la vôtre!* or
Santé!

2 SHOPPING

KEY WORDS AND PHRASES

je voudrais . . .	I'd like . . .
Vous avez . . . ?	Do you have . . . ?
ce sera tout	that will be all
Voulez-vous autre chose?	Would you like something else?
Qu'est-ce que vous voulez?	What would you like?
Avec ceci?	Anything else?
voilà	there you are
C'est combien?	How much is it?
Je vous dois combien?	How much do I owe you?
cela vous fait vingt-deux francs cinquante	That will be 22,50 francs

CONVERSATIONS

BUYING A SIGHTSEEING GUIDE

MARIE-PIERRE	Bonjour, madame.
EMPLOYEE	Bonjour, madame.
MARIE-PIERRE	Un guide du château, s'il vous plaît.
EMPLOYEE	Bien sûr. Celui-ci?
MARIE-PIERRE	Oui, très bien. Merci.

BUYING THE LOCAL LIQUEUR

BEATRICE	Je voudrais une bouteille de cointreau, s'il vous plaît.
VENDEUR	Une bouteille de cointreau. Une grande ou une petite?
BEATRICE	Une grande.
VENDEUR	Une grande bouteille. Eh bien, tenez. Voilà madame.

A BAGUETTE PLEASE

BEATRICE	Bonjour, madame.
MME CHAILLOU	Bonjour, madame.
BEATRICE	Une baguette, s'il vous plaît.
MME CHAILLOU	Oui.
BEATRICE	Merci.
MME CHAILLOU	Voulez-vous autre chose?
BEATRICE	Non merci.

AT THE DELICATESSEN

BEATRICE	Je voudrais du fromage, s'il vous plaît.
MME CHAILLOU	Oui.
BEATRICE	Deux cents grammes de gruyère.
MME CHAILLOU	Bien . . . Avec ceci madame?
BEATRICE	Je voudrais du saucisson, s'il vous plaît.
MME CHAILLOU	Oui.
BEATRICE	Six tranches de celui-là.
MME CHAILLOU	Six tranches de celui-là. Oui. Avec ceci, madame?
BEATRICE	Ce sera tout.

AT THE INDOOR MARKET

BEATRICE	Un kilo de pommes, s'il vous plaît.
VENDEUSE	Oui. Qu'est-ce que vous voulez? Des goldens, des . . . ?

| BEATRICE | Oui, des goldens. |
| VENDEUSE | Des goldens? D'accord. |

BUYING GASOLINE/PETROL

POMPISTE	Bonjour, monsieur-dame.
M. BOUILLON	Bonjour, monsieur. Le plein s'il vous plaît.
POMPISTE	D'essence, de super ou de super sans plomb?
M. BOUILLON	Super sans plomb, s'il vous plaît.
POMPISTE	Merci.

GETTING FRENCH CURRENCY

MARIE-PIERRE	Je voudrais changer des travellers chèques, s'il vous plaît.
EMPLOYEE	Oui. Travellers chèques en francs français?
MARIE-PIERRE	Oui, en francs français.
EMPLOYEE	D'accord. Est-ce que vous avez votre passeport?
MARIE-PIERRE	Oui . . . Voilà!

HOW MUCH IS IT?

MARIE-PIERRE	Vous avez un plan de la ville, s'il vous plaît?
MME HOPPELER	Oui. Voilà.
MARIE-PIERRE	C'est combien?
MME HOPPELER	C'est gratuit.

AT THE POST OFFICE

M. BOUILLON	Bonjour, monsieur.
EMPLOYE	Bonjour.
M. BOUILLON	Pour envoyer une carte postale en Grande-Bretagne, c'est combien s'il vous plaît?
EMPLOYE	C'est deux francs trente.
M. BOUILLON	Très bien. Je voudrais six timbres alors.
EMPLOYE	Voilà.

M. BOUILLON	C'est combien?
EMPLOYE	Treize francs quatre-vingts.

HOW MUCH DO I OWE YOU?

BEATRICE	Je vous dois combien?
MME CHAILLOU	Cela vous fait vingt-deux francs cinquante.
BEATRICE	Oui, *(handing 30 francs)* voilà.
MME CHAILLOU	Oui, merci. Vingt-deux francs cinquante, *(giving the change)* vingt-trois, vingt-quatre, vingt-cinq et trente. Merci. Au revoir, madame.
BEATRICE	Au revoir, madame.

WORD LIST

celui-ci	this one
grand(e)	big
petit(e)	small
eh bien, tenez	here you are
le fromage	cheese
le saucisson (à l'ail)	(garlic) sausage
une tranche	slice
celui-là	that one
le plein	fill it up
l'essence (f)	regular gas
le super	premium
le super sans plomb	premium unleaded
un plan de la ville	map of the town
gratuit(e)	free (of charge)
une carte postale	postcard
la Grande-Bretagne	Great Britain
un timbre	stamp

EXPLANATIONS

SAYING WHAT YOU WANT

The sales assistant may ask:
Qu'est-ce que vous voulez?
Que voulez-vous?
Vous désirez?

Then, like ordering a drink, you can just name what you want and add 'please':
Un guide du château
Une baguette } *s'il vous plaît*
Le plein

You can also say *Je voudrais* . . . (I'd like . . .) or *Vous avez* . . . ? (Do you have . . . ?):
Je voudrais une bouteille de cointreau, s'il vous plaît
Vous avez un plan de la ville?
Vous avez des goldens?

Another way of saying 'I'd like' is *J'aimerais*
J'aimerais six tranches de saucisson, s'il vous plaît

MASCULINE AND FEMININE

You already know *un* and *une* for 'a'/'an'. 'The' is either *le* with a masculine word or *la* with a feminine word:
le guide du château
la bouteille de cointreau

PLURAL

Un and *une* become *des*, while *le* and *la* become *les*:

un *travellers chèque*	**des** *travellers chèques*
une *golden*	**des** *goldens*
la *pomme*	**les** *pommes*
le *guide du château*	**les** *guides du château*

'SOME' AND 'ANY'

'Some' and 'any' are *du, de la, de l'* or *des*. You use *du* with a masculine word, *de la* with a feminine word, *de l'* if the word begins with a vowel. With all plural words, you use *des:*

J'aimerais {
  du fromage
  de l'essence sans plomb
  de la limonade
  des timbres
}

Du, de la, de l' and *des* can also mean 'of the':
Un guide du château, s'il vous plaît
Vous avez un plan de la ville?

HOW MUCH DO YOU WANT?

The assistant may want to know how many (apples) you want or how many slices (of garlic sausage):
Combien en voulez-vous?
Vous voulez combien de tranches?

You might want to reply:

Un kilo de goldens	A kilo of golden delicious apples
Une livre de tomates	A pound of tomatoes
Deux cents grammes de gruyère	Two hundred grammes of gruyère cheese
Une douzaine d'oeufs	A dozen eggs
Une bouteille d'eau minérale	A bottle of mineral water
Un paquet de biscuits	A package of cookies
Une brique de lait	A carton of milk

You may be offered a choice:
Grand ou petit?
Celui-ci or *Celui-là?* with masculine words
Celle-ci or *Celle-là?* with feminine words
Rouge ou blanc?
D'essence, de super ou de super sans plomb?

The assistant is almost bound to ask:
Vous voulez autre chose?
Et avec ceci?   } Anything else?
C'est tout?

If you have all you want, you can reply:
Ce sera tout That will be all

HOW MUCH IS IT?

To find out how much you have to pay, ask:
C'est combien?
Je vous dois combien?

You can also ask:
C'est combien les goldens?
C'est combien la bouteille de cointreau?

NUMBERS

To understand prices in shops you'll need to understand numbers. (You'll find a more detailed list of numbers on page 79.)

vingt	*vingt et un*	*vingt-deux*	*trente*
20	21	22	30
quarante	*cinquante*	*soixante*	*cent*
40	50	60	100

deux cents	*deux cent cinquante*
200	250

PRICES

They are written and spoken as follows:
20,60 F = *vingt francs soixante*
45,60 F = *quarante-cinq francs soixante*
250,30 F = *deux cent cinquante francs trente*

If you don't understand, don't panic. Just ask the assistant to write the price down:
Vous pouvez m'écrire le prix, s'il vous plaît?

EXERCISES

1 HERE'S YOUR SHOPPING LIST

Ask for each of the items on this shopping list, start with *j'aimerais* or *je voudrais* and finish with *s'il vous plaît:*

a 1 bottle of red wine
b 3 loaves of French bread
c 450 grams of gruyère
d 8 slices of (garlic) sausage
e 2 kilos of apples
f 1 pound of tomatoes

2 MIXED UP

You've bought the cheese, the (garlic) sausage and the apples. The sales assistant's side of the conversation is below, but it has been mixed up. Sort out the correct order, and work out the complete conversation.

a Et avec ceci?
b Qu'est-ce que vous voulez?
c Combien de kilos?
d Vous voulez autre chose?
e Combien de tranches?

3 HOW MUCH?

Put the first three prices into figures and the rest into words.

a le vin = vingt-cinq francs soixante
b la baguette = deux francs quatre-vingts

  c le gruyère = quatorze francs trente-trois
  d le saucisson = 15,00 F
  e les pommes = 9,50 F
  f les tomates = 13,29 F

4 AT THE FRUIT MARKET

What's your side of this conversation?

VENDEUSE	Bonjour monsieur.
VOUS	*Greet the stallholder. She's a young woman.*
VENDEUSE	Qu'est-ce que vous voulez?
VOUS	*You'd like a kilo of apples.*
VENDEUSE	Oui . . . Et avec ceci?
VOUS	*Six tomatoes, please.*
VENDEUSE	Voilà.
VOUS	*Thank her and ask how much the oranges are.*
VENDEUSE	Huit francs le kilo.

5 A FEW NECESSITIES

How do you ask for them?

a Your first stop is the tourist office: you'd like a guide of Angers.

b Now to the bank: you'd like to change £200 into French francs (£1 and 1lb are both *une livre*).

c You call at the post office: you'd like four stamps for America.

d Finally, on to the gas station: you'd like 20 liters of unleaded gasoline.

WORTH KNOWING

GASOLINE

Gasoline in France comes in three grades: *essence* or *ordinaire* (regular), *super* (premium), and *essence sans plomb* (unleaded). You'll also come across *superplus* (super-premium) and *super sans plomb* (premium unleaded).

MONEY

The *franc* (F) is divided into 100 *centimes* (c). You'll find coins of 5 c, 10 c, 20 c, ½ F, 1 F, 2 F, 5 F and 10 F. There are notes for 20 F, 50 F, 100 F, 200 F and 500 F. In shops, your bills will be rounded off to the nearest multiple of five centimes. For example, 54,27 F becomes only 54,25 F!

BREAD

There's a large variety of breads in France, all worth trying. To help you, here are a few names:

la ficelle	smaller and thinner than the baguette
la boule	a round loaf
la couronne	a loaf in the shape of a crown
le pain paillasse	leavened bread
le pain de seigle	rye bread
le pain complet	whole wheat bread
le pain aux céréales	whole wheat bread made with different sorts of grain
le pain de campagne	farmhouse bread

If you ask for *un pain* you'll be given a stick of white bread (also called *un parisien*) roughly equivalent to two baguettes.

SHOPS

You might find it useful to know the following shops:

la boucherie	butcher's
la boulangerie	baker's
la charcuterie	delicatessen
l'épicerie (f)	grocer's
la maison de la presse	newsstand
la pharmacie	drugstore
le tabac	tobacconist's

If you don't want to go to the trouble of cooking a meal, the *charcuterie* may have all you need. There you'll find ready-prepared dishes, both hot and cold.

3 GETTING AROUND

KEY WORDS AND PHRASES

Le centre-ville, s'il vous plaît?	The town center, please?
Il y un parking près d'ici?	Is there a parking lot nearby?
Pour aller à la cathédrale?	How do I get to the cathedral?
à droite	on/to the right
à gauche	on/to the left
là-bas	over there
vous prenez . . .	you take . . .
la première rue à droite	the first road on the right
la deuxième à gauche	the second on the left
tout droit	straight ahead
Quelle heure est-il?	what time is it?
A quelle heure ferme le château?	what time does the castle close?
C'est ouvert quand?	when is it open?
un aller simple	a one-way ticket
un aller-retour	a round-trip ticket

CONVERSATIONS

THE TOWN CENTER, PLEASE.

MARIE-PIERRE	Pardon, monsieur.
PASSANT	Oui.
MARIE-PIERRE	Le centre-ville, s'il vous plaît?
PASSANT	Alors, c'est très facile. Vous prenez la

deuxième à gauche . . .

MARIE-PIERRE	Oui.
PASSANT	Et ensuite c'est tout droit.

AND IS IT FAR FROM HERE?

MARIE-PIERRE	Et c'est loin d'ici?
PASSANT	Non. Environ deux minutes à pied.
MARIE-PIERRE	D'accord, merci beaucoup. Au revoir, monsieur.
PASSANT	Je vous en prie. Au revoir.

IS THERE A BANK NEARBY?

MARIE-PIERRE	Excusez-moi, monsieur. Il y a une banque près d'ici?
PASSANT	Une banque . . . Oui, le Crédit Lyonnais est là-bas, la deuxième rue à droite.
MARIE-PIERRE	Et c'est loin d'ici?
PASSANT	Oh, non. C'est à deux cents mètres.
MARIE-PIERRE	D'accord. Merci beaucoup.
PASSANT	De rien.
MARIE-PIERRE	Au revoir, monsieur.
PASSANT	Au revoir.

SORRY, I'M NOT FROM HERE!

PIERRICK	Pardon, madame. Il y a un parking près d'ici?
PASSANTE	Ah, désolée. Je ne suis pas d'ici.
PIERRICK	Ah, ça ne fait rien. Merci.

LOOKING FOR A GAS STATION

PIERRICK	Pardon, madame. Il y a une station d'essence près d'ici?
PASSANTE	Oui. Vous prenez sur votre droite . . .
PIERRICK	Oui.
PASSANTE	Et la station est tout de suite à gauche.
PIERRICK	Et c'est loin, non?
PASSANTE	Non, à peu près cinq cents mètres.

HOW DO I GET TO THE CATHEDRAL, PLEASE?

MARIE-PIERRE	Pardon, madame. Pour aller à la cathédrale, s'il vous plaît?
MME CHAILLOU	Pour aller à la cathédrale . . . Alors, de la rue Bressigny, vous traversez le boulevard Foch.
MARIE-PIERRE	Oui.
MME CHAILLOU	Vous suivez la rue Saint Aubin, la rue piétonne.
MARIE-PIERRE	Oui.
MME CHAILLOU	Et vous arrivez à la cathédrale.

AT THE TOURIST INFORMATION OFFICE

MARIE-PIERRE	Le musée David d'Angers, c'est où?
MME HOPPELER	Eh bien, il est tout près d'ici, sur votre droite.
MARIE-PIERRE	Et c'est ouvert quand, s'il vous plaît?
MME HOPPELER	C'est ouvert tous les jours . . .
MARIE-PIERRE	Mmmn . . .
MME HOPPELER	De neuf heures à douze heures et de quatorze heures à dix-huit heures.

TWO TICKETS FOR THE CASTLE, PLEASE

PIERRICK	Deux tickets pour le château, s'il vous plaît.
EMPLOYEE	Oui. Voilà. Quarante-six francs, s'il vous plaît.
PIERRICK	Voilà.
EMPLOYEE	Merci. Alors quarante-six, quarante-huit, cinquante; une, deux, trois, quatre et cinq qui vous font cent.
PIERRICK	Merci beaucoup. Et à quelle heure ferme le château?
EMPLOYEE	Dix-sept heures trente.

WHAT'S THE TIME, PLEASE?

MARIE-PIERRE	Pardon, monsieur. Quelle heure est-il, s'il vous plaît?
PASSANT	Il est trois heures moins dix.
MARIE-PIERRE	Merci.
PASSANT	Je vous en prie.

BUYING TRAIN TICKETS

PIERRICK	Je voudrais deux aller-retour pour Nantes s'il vous plaît.
EMPLOYE	Oui monsieur. En première ou en seconde classe?
PIERRICK	En seconde, s'il vous plaît.
EMPLOYE	Bien monsieur. Voilà. Deux cent huit francs, s'il vous plaît.
PIERRICK	Voilà.
EMPLOYE	Je vous remercie.

A ONE-WAY TICKET TO PARIS

MARIE-PIERRE	Je voudrais un aller simple pour Paris, s'il vous plaît.
EMPLOYE	Oui. En première ou en seconde classe?
MARIE-PIERRE	En seconde classe.
EMPLOYE	Bien. Cent cinquante-quatre francs, s'il vous plaît.

WORD LIST

facile	easy
ensuite	then
environ	about
à pied	on foot
je vous en prie	my pleasure/you're welcome
là-bas	(over) there

à deux cents mètres	200 meters away
la station d'essence	gas station
vous prenez sur votre droite	you turn right
tout de suite à gauche	just on the left
à peu près cinq cents mètres	about 500 meters
alors	well
de la rue Bressigny	from the rue Bressigny
vous traversez	you cross
vous suivez	you follow
la rue piétonne	the pedestrian street
tout près d'ici	very near here
sur votre droite	on your right
qui vous font cent	which make 100
en première ou en seconde classe?	first or second class?

EXPLANATIONS

ASKING THE WAY

The simplest way is to name the place you want to get to and add 'please':

le centre-ville
la cathédrale } *s'il vous plaît?*
le musée

You can also start with *pour aller à . . . .:*

à la cathédrale
au château
Pour aller à l'hôtel } *s'il vous plaît?*
aux toilettes
à Nantes

Notice that you use *à la* if the word is feminine, *au* (= *à + le*) if it's masculine, *à l'* if it begins with a vowel or an 'h' which is not pronounced, and *aux* (= *à + les*) if it's plural.

To stop a passer-by in the street, say:

Pardon, monsieur
Excusez-moi, madame } *le centre-ville, s'il vous plaît?*

If you want to know where a place is, the key word is *où:*
Le musée, c'est où?
C'est où la gare, s'il vous plaît?
Où est le musée, s'il vous plaît?

To ask how far or near the place is, say:
C'est loin d'ici?
Il y a une pharmacie près d'ici?

The answer is likely to include a time or a distance:
Non, environ deux minutes à pied No, about two minutes' walk
Oh, non. C'est à deux cents mètres Oh no. It's 200 meters away
C'est à une heure en voiture It's an hour's drive away

DIRECTIONS

No matter how you travel, the basic directions are the same:

tout droit straight ahead
la première à droite first right
la deuxième sur votre gauche the second on your left

Here are some more useful expressions. On the map below,
follow the directions given overleaf.

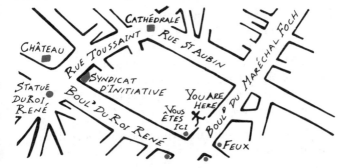

You're on the Boulevard du Maréchal Foch.
- *Pour aller à la cathédrale, s'il vous plaît?*
- *Vous prenez* (take) *la première rue sur votre gauche et vous continuez tout droit. La cathédrale est devant* (in front) *vous.*
- *Pour aller au château, s'il vous plaît?*
- *Vous tournez à droite aux feux* (traffic lights). *Puis vous allez tout droit jusqu'à* (as far as) *la statue du Roi René* (the statue of King René). *Et voilà, le château!*
- *Pour aller au syndicat d'initiative, s'il vous plaît?*
- *Le syndicat d'initiative? C'est juste à côté* (next to) *du château*

FIRST, SECOND, THIRD . . .

'First' is *premier* with a masculine word or *première* with a feminine word. Otherwise you normally add -*ième* to the cardinal number: *deux**ième**, trois**ième.***

There are three exceptions, however. With *vingt et un, trente et un,* etc., 'first' becomes -*unième*, producing *vingt et unième, trente et unième,* etc. An 'e' at the end of the cardinal number is dropped: *quatre* becomes *quatrième, onze* becomes *onzième.* Finally the 'f' at the end of *neuf* becomes *v*, producing *neuvième.*

WHAT'S THE TIME

To find out what the time is, ask: *Quelle heure est-il?*

To tell someone the time, start with *Il est:*

Il est huit heures	It's eight o'clock
huit heures cinq	five past . . .
huit heures et quart	quarter past . . .
huit heures et demie	half past . . .
huit heures moins le quart	quarter to . . .
huit heures moins dix	ten to . . .

The 24-hour clock is also frequently used, and not only in official situations:

Le train part à quinze heures seize (15:16)
Il arrive à dix-huit heures trente-neuf (18:39)

In the 24-hour clock, midday is *douze heures* and midnight is
zéro heure:
Le train part à douze heures quinze
Il arrive à zéro heure neuf

Otherwise, it's either *midi* (midday) or *minuit* (midnight);
a.m. is *du matin (il est dix heures du matin);* p.m. is *de l'après-midi*
till 6 p.m. or *du soir* thereafter *(il est cinq heures de l'après-midi/il
est neuf heures du soir).*

WHAT TIME DOES IT OPEN/CLOSE?

To ask when a place opens or closes:
A quelle heure ouvre la pharmacie?
A quelle heure ferme la banque?

You can also say:
Le musée, c'est ouvert quand?

To find out whether a place is open or shut, just say:
C'est ouvert? C'est fermé?

GOING BY TRAIN

To buy a train ticket, say for example:
Un aller-simple pour Le Mans en seconde, s'il vous plaît
A second-class single to Le Mans, please
un aller-simple a one-way/single
un aller-retour a round-trip/return
pour (Nantes, Paris) to (Nantes, Paris)
en première first class
en seconde second class

To inquire whether there's a train for Nantes at 8:00:
Il y a un train pour Nantes à huit heures?
To inquire about train departures:
A quelle heure part le train pour Nantes?
To find out at what time the train arrives:
Il arrive à quelle heure?
To find out which platform the train leaves from:
C'est quel quai pour . . . ?

DAYS OF THE WEEK

Starting with Sunday, they are:
dimanche, lundi, mardi, mercredi, jeudi, vendredi, samedi

Note that in French, initial capital letters are not needed.

EXERCISES

1 DIRECTIONS

Work out the questions and answers using the map and
prompts below.

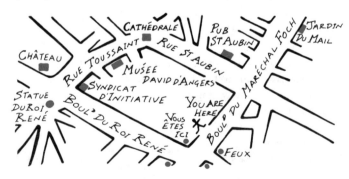

EXAMPLE

You want to go from the Jardin du Mail to the Pub St Aubin.

— *Pour aller du Jardin du Mail au Pub St Aubin, s'il vous plaît?*
— *Vous prenez le Boulevard du Maréchal Foch sur la gauche et vous tournez dans la quatrième rue à droite.*

You want to go . . .
a   From the cathedral to the castle.
b   From the Tourist Information Office to the Jardin du Mail.
c   From the Pub St Aubin to the Musée David d'Angers.

2   WHAT TIME IS IT?

How would you say each of these times in French?

a   10:25 a.m. b   1:40 p.m. c   4:05 a.m. d   9:30 p.m.
e   15:10   f   13:15   g   21:35   h   00:42

3   HOW DO I GET TO . . . ?

You stop a passer-by to ask the way to the castle. What do you say?

VOUS   *Excuse-me.*
PASSANT   Oui?
VOUS   *How do I get to the castle, please?*
PASSANT   C'est très facile. Vous prenez le boulevard du Maréchal Foch jusqu'au boulevard du Roi René, sur votre droite . . .
VOUS   *Sorry. More slowly, please.*
PASSANT   Alors tout droit. Puis le boulevard du Roi René à droite.
VOUS   *On the left . . . the boulevard of the Roi René . . .*
PASSANT   Non. A droite. Et c'est tout droit.
VOUS   *OK. And is it far?*
PASSANT   Non. Dix minutes à pied.
VOUS   *Fine. Thank you very much.*
PASSANT   Je vous en prie.
VOUS   *Goodbye.*

4 BUYING TRAIN TICKETS

What would you say to buy the following tickets?

EXAMPLE *Un aller simple pour Tours, en seconde.*

You're now making inquiries about going to Saumur.

d Ask whether there's a train for Saumur at 10:00.
e Ask which platform the train leaves from.
f Ask how much a first–class round-trip ticket is.

5 OPENING AND CLOSING TIMES

When can you visit each of these places?

a *Musée:* ouvert de 10 h jusqu'à 17 h 30; fermé le dimanche.
b *Château:* ouvert de 9 h 30 jusqu'à 18 h; fermé le lundi.
c *Cathédrale:* ouvert tous les jours de 9 h jusqu'à 18 h.

WORTH KNOWING

TRAVELING BY ROAD, BY TRAIN AND ON FOOT

Roads in France are divided into three main categories:
"A": *autoroute* (superhighway)
"N": *nationale* (highway)
"D": *départementale* (secondary road)

In summer, main French roads can be very busy. Each year, the French authorities run a special information service called

Bison Futé (the cunning buffalo) to help holidaymakers avoid congested areas (*les points noirs*) and traffic jams (*les bouchons*). They recommend alternative routes called *Itinéraires Bis* and relief routes called *Itinéraires de délestage*. You can get maps at service stations or toll booths on the highway. Information is also given on the radio.

Here are some useful driving expressions:

priorité à droite give way to the right   *travaux* road construction
stationnement interdit no parking   *déviation* detour
chaussée déformée uneven road surface
horodateur parking meter

As an alternative to driving, you may want to take the train. France's railway network is the SNCF (*Société Nationale des Chemins de Fer français*); trains are generally modern and comfortable, with a well-stocked buffet car—and are invariably on time, too. You could try the TGV (*train à grande vitesse*), France's high-speed train. You'll need to buy your seat in advance and pay a small booking fee (*un supplément*).

In the railway station itself, look out for the following signs: *GUICHET* (ticket office), *RENSEIGNEMENTS* (information office), *DEPARTS ET ARRIVEES* (departures and arrivals), *SALLE D'ATTENTE* (waiting room), *CONSIGNE* (check room), and *ACCES AUX QUAIS* (access to platforms).

Before getting on any train, your ticket must be validated (*composter*): *le compostage du ticket* is compulsory if you don't want to be fined.

If you want to explore France at a more leisurely pace, you may choose to travel on *les sentiers* or *les chemins de grande randonnée* (long-distance footpaths) and stay at a *gîte d'étapes* (night stop-over houses). On maps, the long-distance footpaths are indicated '*GR*' followed by a number (*GR2*) for example.

4 FINDING SOMEWHERE TO STAY

KEY WORDS AND PHRASES

Vous avez . . .	Do you have . . .
des chambres de libre?	rooms available
de la place de libre	space available (in campsite)
Je voudrais réserver . . .	I'd like to make a reservation . . .
une chambre à un grand lit	a room with a double bed
avec douche/bain/cabinet de toilette	with shower/bath/washing facilities
J'ai . . .	I have . . .
une réservation	a reservation
une caravane/une tente	a mobile home/a tent
pour ce soir	for tonight
pour la semaine prochaine	for next week
pour trois nuits	for three nights
du trois au six mai	from May 3 to 6
je voudrais la clef numéro neuf	I'd like key number 9
A quelle heure est-ce que vous servez le petit déjeuner?	What time do you serve breakfast?

CONVERSATIONS

DO YOU HAVE ROOMS AVAILABLE?

PIERRICK	Bonsoir, monsieur.
M. OCHER	Bonsoir, monsieur.

PIERRICK — Vous avez des chambres de libre s'il vous plaît?

M. OCHER — Pour ce soir?

PIERRICK — Oui, pour ce soir.

M. OCHER — Oui, monsieur. Bien sûr. Que désirez-vous? Une chambre avec bain, douche ou cabinet de toilette?

PIERRICK — Avec douche, s'il vous plaît.

WHAT TIME DO YOU SERVE BREAKFAST?

PIERRICK — A quelle heure est-ce que vous servez le petit déjeuner, s'il vous plaît?

M. OCHER — A partir de sept heures.

PIERRICK — Jusqu'à quelle heure?

M. OCHER — Jusqu'à dix heures.

PIERRICK — D'accord. Merci.

MAKING A RESERVATION

PIERRICK — Je voudrais réserver une chambre à un grand lit, s'il vous plaît, pour la semaine prochaine.

M. OCHER — Oui, monsieur. Que désirez-vous? Avec bain, douche ou cabinet de toilette?

PIERRICK — Avec bain, s'il vous plaît.

M. OCHER — Avec bain. Pour quelles dates?

PIERRICK — Du trois au six mai, s'il vous plaît.

CHECKING THE PRICE

PIERRICK — Et c'est combien?

M. OCHER — Deux cent dix francs pour une personne, deux cent vingt francs pour deux personnes.

PIERRICK — Et le petit déjeuner est compris?

M. OCHER — Non, en supplément, vingt-quatre francs.

PIERRICK — D'accord. Ça va.

SPELLING YOUR NAME

M. OCHER — Quel est votre nom?

PIERRICK	Alors, je m'appelle Monsieur Picot. P-I-C-O-T.
M. OCHER	Monsieur Picot. Très bien, monsieur. C'est inscrit.
PIERRICK	Je vous remercie.

ARRIVING AT THE HOTEL

MARIE-PIERRE	Bonjour, monsieur.
M. OCHER	Bonjour, madame.
MARIE-PIERRE	J'ai une réservation, je crois.
M. OCHER	Oui, pour ce soir?
MARIE-PIERRE	Oui, pour ce soir.
M. OCHER	On va regarder. Quel est votre nom?
MARIE-PIERRE	Méchineau.
M. OCHER	Ah, oui. Madame Méchineau. Vous avez la chambre numéro neuf, madame. Au deuxième étage.
MARIE-PIERRE	D'accord.

IS THERE A MESSAGE FOR ME?

PIERRICK	Est-ce qu'il y a un message pour moi?
M. OCHER	Non, il n'y a pas de message, monsieur.
PIERRICK	Rien du tout?
M. OCHER	Rien du tout.
PIERRICK	Ça ne fait rien.

ASKING FOR THE KEY

MARIE-PIERRE	Bonsoir, monsieur.
M. OCHER	Bonsoir, madame.
MARIE-PIERRE	Je voudrais la clef pour la chambre numéro neuf, s'il vous plaît.
M. OCHER	Voici, madame.
MARIE-PIERRE	Merci.

STAYING AN EXTRA NIGHT

MARIE-PIERRE	Vous avez une chambre pour ce soir?

M. OCHER	Oh non, malheureusement. Nous sommes complets, madame.
MARIE-PIERRE	Ah! Bon. Tant pis!

PAYING THE BILL

MARIE-PIERRE	Je peux vous payer?
M. OCHER	Oui, bien sûr. Je vais préparer votre note, madame.
MARIE-PIERRE	D'accord.
M. OCHER	Alors c'est la chambre numéro neuf?
MARIE-PIERRE	Oui.
M. OCHER	Vous avez trois nuits à cent quatre-vingt-quinze francs, cinq cent quatre-vingt-cinq francs.
MARIE-PIERRE	Oui.
M. OCHER	Trois petits déjeuners, soixante-douze francs. Pas de téléphone?
MARIE-PIERRE	Pas de téléphone, non, non.
M. OCHER	Alors ça vous fait sept . . . quinze . . . six cent cinquante-cinq francs. (He's rounding it down.)

CHECKING IN AT THE CAMPSITE

PIERRICK	Vous avez de la place, s'il vous plaît?
RECEPTIONNISTE	Bien sûr, oui. C'est pour une nuit, monsieur?
PIERRICK	Non, pour trois nuits.
RECEPTIONNISTE	Ah, pour trois nuits. Oui. Alors, vous avez une caravane ou une tente?
PIERRICK	Une caravane.
RECEPTIONNISTE	Oui. Vous êtes combien de personnes?
PIERRICK	Quatre personnes. Deux adultes et deux enfants. Et c'est combien la nuit?
RECEPTIONNISTE	Alors, ça vous fera quarante-sept francs cinquante pour quatre personnes, plus l'électricité vingt-trois francs cinquante.

WORD LIST

à partir de	from
jusqu'à	until/up to
Pour quelles dates?	For which dates?
c'est possible	it's possible
je m'appelle . . .	my name is . . .
c'est inscrit	it's booked
on va regarder	we'll have a look
Quel est votre nom?	What's your name?
numéro neuf	number nine
au deuxième étage	on the second floor
malheureusement	unfortunately
tant pis	never mind
Je peux vous payer?	Can I pay you?
je vais préparer votre note	I'll just prepare your bill
ça vous fait . . .	That's . . .
un enfant	a child
ça vous fera . . .	That will be

EXPLANATIONS

RESERVING A ROOM OR CAMPSITE

To ask if any rooms/spaces are available:

Vous avez $\begin{cases} \textit{des chambres de libre?} \\ \textit{une chambre pour ce soir?} \\ \textit{de la place, s'il vous plaît?} \end{cases}$

To specify which kind of room:

Je voudrais une chambre $\begin{cases} \textit{avec bain/douche/cabinet de toilette} \\ \textit{à or avec un grand lit} \\ \textit{à deux lits} \\ \textit{avec un petit lit d'enfant} \end{cases}$

At the campsite, say:

Nous avons $\left\{\begin{array}{l} \textit{une tente} \\ \textit{une caravane} \\ \textit{une canadienne} \text{ (a small ridge tent)} \end{array}\right.$

Checking in at the hotel:
J'ai une réservation

FOR HOW LONG?

When making your booking, you will be asked how long you want to stay:
Pour quelles dates? For which dates?
Pour combien de nuits? For how many nights?
Pour combien de temps? For how long?

To give the length of your stay, say:
Pour une nuit For one night
Pour quatre nuits For four nights
Pour une semaine For a week

From . . . to . . .
You can say *de . . . à* or *à partir de . . . jusqu'à . . .*:
A partir de sept heures jusqu'à dix heures
To give the exact dates, use *du . . . au* or *à partir du . . . jusqu'au . . . .*
Du trois au six mai or *à partir du trois mai jusqu'au six mai*.

HOW MUCH IS IT?

To ask how much the room is, say:
C'est combien la chambre?
C'est combien la chambre avec douche/bain s'il vous plaît?

If you want to ask whether breakfast is included:
Le petit déjeuner est compris?

Most of the time, it won't be included and the receptionist will answer:
Non, c'est en supplément or *en plus* or *en sus*, which means 'No, it's extra'.

NO, THERE'S NO MESSAGE

To say 'there isn't . . .' or that something 'is not so', you use
ne and *pas*. They usually come either side of the verb:
Non, je ne suis pas d'Angers
Ce n'est pas possible

With *il y a,* however, *ne* comes before the *y:*
Non, il n'y a pas de message, monsieur

In spoken French, the *ne* often gets lost, so you'll hear, for
example:
Je 'suis pas d'Angers
C'est pas possible
'Y a pas de message
'Pas de téléphone

SPELLING YOUR NAME

It can be very useful to know how to spell your name. To
practise, listen to the cassette and have a look at the
pronunciation guide (page 76). If, like Pierrick, you have a
double letter in your name, use *deux* to say double:

P-I-E-deux R-I-C-K

EXERCISES

1   RESERVING HOTEL ROOMS

Ask for each of the following:

a   two rooms with a double bed and a bath for three nights
b   one room with twin beds and a shower for tonight
c   one single room with washing facilities from August
9 to 12
d   one room with double bed and a child's bed, with shower,
for next week
e   one room with a shower for one child and one room with
a bath for two adults

2 MIX AND MATCH

Match the questions with the correct answers.

1 Est-ce que vous avez des chambres de libre?
2 Le petit déjeuner est compris?
3 Il y a un message pour moi, s'il vous plaît?
4 C'est pour combien de nuits?

a Rien du tout monsieur.   **c** Oui, monsieur.
b Pour six nuits.   **d** Non, c'est en plus.

3 SPEAKING TO THE RECEPTIONIST

Ask the hotel receptionist:

a if they've got any rooms available
b the price of a room with washing facilities
c if breakfast is included
d at what time breakfast is served

4 THERE MUST BE SOME MISTAKE!

You've made a reservation, but there's been a mistake and the hotel is full. What do you say?

VOUS	*Good evening*
RECEPTIONNISTE	Bonsoir, monsieur-dame.
VOUS	*Say you've got a reservation for a room with a double bed and a shower.*
RECEPTIONNISTE	Oui, c'est quel nom, s'il vous plaît?
VOUS	*Tell him your name's Stuart.*
RECEPTIONNISTE	Mmm. . . Stuart. Non. Je suis désolé. Il n'y a pas de chambre dans votre nom.
VOUS	*Say you don't understand.*
RECEPTIONNISTE	Non, monsieur-dame. Je suis désolé,
VOUS	*Ask if there's another hotel nearby.*
RECEPTIONNISTE	Oui, il y a l'Hôtel de France. Je vais téléphoner pour vous.
VOUS	*Thank him.*

5　FILL IN THE BLANKS

Can you fill in this campsite form using the information below?

Your name is Liz Paine; you are staying for seven nights from July 23; your vehicle number is—789 ABC; you have one mobile home and one tent; there are two adults and three children; electricity is required; your passport number is 934507 D.

CAMPING MUNICIPAL DU LAC DE MAINE
FICHE DE RENSEIGNEMENTS

Nom: ....

Prénom: ....

Numéro du passeport: ....

Numéro d'immatriculation du véhicule: ....

Nombre de personnes: .... adultes ....

enfants ....

Caravane: ....

Tente: ....

Electricité: (oui/non) ....

Nombres de nuits: ....

Dates: ....

WORTH KNOWING

In France, hotels are graded from one to five stars. Some have the letters 'NN' (*nouvelles normes*) after the stars, as well as the relevant year. The Hôtel du Mail, for example, displays '★★ NN 1990'. Yearly classification ensures that hotels comply with the grading specifications.

An alternative to hotels is the continental B&B, known as *une chambre d'hôte*. Sometimes, owners also offer a *table d'hôte,* which means that you can have your evening meal there too. In popular areas, you may need to book in advance. Ask the local tourist office (*le syndicat d'initiative*), which will give you all the relevant information.

Renting a *gîte* can also be an ideal way of spending a holiday in France. *Gîtes* are self-catering accommodations, ranging from cottages to flats, graded with one to three ears of corn.

Campsites are also rated from one to four stars according to the facilities they offer. Most towns and villages will have their *camping municipal*. You can also try *le camping à la ferme;* these campsites are run by local farmers who rent one of their fields close to the farm. They tend to be very small and offer only basic facilities, but an attraction is the fresh farm produce (*produits de la ferme*) such as eggs (*oeufs*), milk (*lait*) and vegetables (*légumes*), which are often readily available.

5 EATING OUT

Est-ce que vous avez une table pour trois, s'il vous plaît?	Do you have a table for three, please?
Vous prenez un menu ou la carte?	Will you have a set meal or choose from the à la carte list?
Vous avez choisi?	Have you chosen?
en/comme entrée	as a starter
trois menus à cent vingt, s'il vous plaît	three set meals at 120,00 F (each), please
la carte, s'il vous plaît	the menu, please
avec les escargots	with the snails
un Anjou blanc	a white Anjou
l'addition, s'il vous plaît	the bill, please

CONVERSATIONS

ASKING FOR THE MENU

PIERRICK	Excusez-moi!
M. MENARD	Oui?
PIERRICK	La carte, s'il vous plaît.
M. MENARD	Voilà, monsieur.

SET MEAL OR A LA CARTE?

PIERRICK	Marie-Pierre, vous prenez un menu ou à la carte?
MARIE-PIERRE	Je vais prendre un menu à soixante.

A LA CARTE . . .

PIERRICK	Qu'est-ce que vous prenez, Marie-Pierre?
MARIE-PIERRE	Un bon steak saignant pour moi.
PIERRICK	Et comme légumes? Des pommes frites, des haricots verts, des flageolets . . . ?
MARIE PIERRE	Des pommes frites. Des pommes frites et une salade verte.
PIERRICK	Et pour moi, un bon steak à point et des haricots verts.

AT THE PATISSERIE

MME GABORIAU	Comme pâtisseries, monsieur-dame?
MARIE-PIERRE	Hmmn . . .
MME GABORIAU	Une viennoiserie, une spécialité?
MARIE-PIERRE	Non, un pain au chocolat pour moi.
MME GABORIAU	Oui, Chaud? froid?
MARIE-PIERRE	Chaud.
MME GABORIAU	Chaud, d'accord. Et pour monsieur?
PIERRICK	Un pain aux raisins, s'il vous plaît.
MME GABORIAU	Chaud également?
PIERRICK	Oui, s'il vous plaît.

ASKING FOR A TABLE

MARC	Bonsoir, monsieur.
M. VEGER	Bonsoir, messieurs-dame.
MARIE-PIERRE	Bonsoir, monsieur.
PIERRICK	Bonsoir, monsieur.
MARC	Est-ce que vous avez une table pour trois personnes, s'il vous plaît?
M. VEGER	Oui, bien sûr.

AN APERITIF?

M. VEGER	Désirez-vous prendre des apéritifs, messieurs-dame?
MARC	Oui, certainement.
PIERRICK	Oui, bien sûr.
MARIE-PIERRE	Oui.
M. VEGER	Nous faisons des kirs au muscadet à la crème de pêche, crème de mûre, crème de cassis, ricard, cinquante et un, martini . . .
MARC	Marie-Pierre?
MARIE-PIERRE	Eh bien, un kir royal, s'il vous plaît.
M. VEGER	Oui.
PIERRICK	Et pour moi, un petit whisky.
MARC	Et un ricard.

ORDERING A SET MEAL

M. VEGER	Avez-vous choisi, messieurs-dame?
TOUS	Oui.
MARC	Alors, trois menus à cent vingt, s'il vous plaît . . .
M. VEGER	Bien, monsieur. En entrée, vous prendrez?
MARC	. . . avec en entrée, trois escargots . . .
M. VEGER	Trois escargots, oui.
MARC	Puis deux filets mignons, et Marie-Pierre?
MARIE-PIERRE	Une sole meunière pour moi.

SOME WINE?

M. VEGER	Avez-vous choisi les vins, messieurs-dame?
MARC	Oui. Alors avec les escargots, un Anjou blanc.
M. VEGER	Oui.
MARC	Et ensuite un Chinon, s'il vous plaît.
M. VEGER	Bien, monsieur.

ORDERING DESSERT

M. VEGER	Qu'est-ce que vous avez choisi comme desserts, messieurs-dame?
MARIE-PIERRE	Eh bien, une Forêt-Noire au chocolat pour moi.
M. VEGER	Oui, madame.
PIERRICK	Pour moi, une . . . pêche melba.
M. VEGER	Oui, monsieur.
MARC	Et moi, une Forêt-Noire aussi.

COFFEES OR LIQUEURS?

M. VEGER	Messieurs-dame, désirez-vous prendre des cafés ou des digestifs?
MARC	Ah, des cafés, oui. Un, deux, trois?
MARIE-PIERRE	Un café pour moi, oui.
PIERRICK	Non, pas pour moi, merci.
MARC	Alors deux cafés, s'il vous plaît. Et est-ce que vous voulez un digestif?
PIERRICK	Un petit cognac pour moi.
MARC	Et un cointreau pour moi.
M. VEGER	Bien, monsieur.

THE BILL, PLEASE

MARC	S'il vous plaît!
M. VEGER	Oui, monsieur?
MARC	L'addition, s'il vous plaît.
M. VEGER	Bien sûr, monsieur.

WORD LIST

je vais prendre	I'm going to have
saignant(e)	rare (steak)
les pommes frites (f)	French fries
les haricots verts (m)	green beans
les flageolets (m)	dwarf kidney beans
une salade verte	green salad
à point	medium (steak)
les pâtisseries (f)	cakes and pastries
la viennoiserie	Viennese pastry
la spécialité	specialty
le pain au chocolat	pastry with chocolate in the middle
le pain au raisins	pastry with raisins
également	also
certainement	certainly
nous faisons des kirs	normally we do kirs (a kir is white wine with blackcurrant liqueur although you may be offered alternative liqueurs)
la crème de pêche	peach liqueur
la crème de mûre	blackberry liqueur
la crème de cassis	blackcurrant liqueur
le cinquante et un	aniseed-based aperitif
le ricard	aniseed-based aperitif
Eh bien	Well
un kir royal	champagne or sparkling wine with (normally) blackcurrant liqueur
En entrée, vous prendrez?	What will you have as a starter?
le filet mignon	beef fillet
la sole meunière	sole fried in butter, served with lemon and parsley
ensuite	then

EXPLANATIONS

THE WAITER'S QUESTIONS

To take your order, the waiter may ask:
Vous avez choisi?
Qu'est-ce que vous désirez?
Qu'est-ce que vous prenez?
Replies:
Le menu à cent vingt
Un kir royal
Le menu à soixante

Then the waiter will ask you about the appetizer, the main dish, and the wine:
Comme entrée? or, less commonly, *en entrée?*
Et comme plat principal?
Et comme vin?
Some replies:
Trois escargots
Deux filets mignons
Un Anjou blanc

To find out about your main course, the waiter may ask:
Et comme poisson? (fish)
Et comme viande? (meat)
Replies:
Une sole meunière
Un bon steak saignant

GETTING A TABLE

To ask for a table and to say how many of you there are:
Une table pour trois personnes s'il vous plaît
Une table pour trois

Restaurants have one or two set meals (*menus*) displayed with the prices and the à la carte list.

If you've chosen a set meal, give the number of people wanting it and its price:

Deux menus à cent vingt-cinq (125,00 F)

If you've decided to eat à la carte, you'll have to answer the waiter's questions (see above) or say:

Alors, comme entrée, je vais prendre/je voudrais les escargots et comme plat principal la sole meunière

If you're not quite sure what a particular dish is, ask:

Qu'est-ce que c'est?

ABOUT QUESTIONS

A statement can also be a question, depending on the intonation used. Raising the intonation at the end of a sentence turns it into a question:

Vous avez une table pour trois?
Vous prenez un/l'apéritif?

You can also begin with *Est-ce que . . . :*

Est-ce que vous avez une table pour trois?
Est-ce que vous voulez un digestif?

Some questions begin with the verb:

Avez-vous une table pour trois?
Avez-vous choisi les vins?

Others begin with a question word:

Que désirez-vous?
Qu'est-ce que c'est?
Où est le restaurant La Treille?

THE BILL, PLEASE

To ask for the bill, say:

L'addition, s'il vous plaît!

If you want to know whether a tip is included, ask:

Le service est compris?

FLAVORS AND INGREDIENTS

These are usually positioned after *au (= à + le)*, *à la* or *aux (= à + les)*:

un pain au chocolat
un pain aux raisins
un kir à la crème de pêche
un kir à la crème de cassis
un sandwich au jambon (ham sandwich)

ADJECTIVES

Adjectives usually come after the noun they describe:

un Anjou blanc
un steak saignant
un kir royal

A few very common ones come before the noun:

un bon steak
un petit cognac
un grand lit

Most adjectives describing feminine nouns add an *e:*

une Forêt-Noire
une salade verte
une grande bouteille

In the plural, adjectives normally take an *-s* at the end (but remember, there are many exceptions):

deux steaks saignants
trois salades vertes

EXERCISES

1 WHICH WOULD YOU CHOOSE?

1 You'd like a snack:
   a un kir royal   **b** un escargot   **c** un sandwich au jambon

2 You've given up alcohol:
   a un citron pressé **b** un cinquante et un **c** un ricard
3 You don't eat meat:
   a un steak saignant **b** un filet mignon
   c une sole meunière
4 You had a huge meal but can't resist a light sweet:
   a une Forêt-Noire **b** une pêche melba
   c une glace à la vanille
5 You want something to warm you up:
   a un pain au chocolat chaud **b** un gâteau à la crème
   c un pain aux raisins

2 WHAT DID THEY ORDER?

What did Marc, Marie-Pierre and Pierrick order at La Treille?
Read the conversations again and make a list in French of the
aperitifs, starters, etc. ordered by each person, starting with the
aperitif, and continuing with the appetizer, etc.

3 IN A RESTAURANT

Ask for:
a A table for three, please.
b One set meal at 75,00 F and two at 140,00 F.
c A vermouth, a whiskey, and a white wine and blackcurrant
       liqueur for me.
d Two steaks (one rare, one medium) and one sole fried in
       butter.
e One bottle of white Anjou.
f Three peach melbas.
g Two black coffees and a white one.
h The bill, please.

4 FILL THE GAPS

a   un sandwich . . . saucisson
b   un gâteau . . . crème
c   un thé . . . citron
d   une glace . . . vanille
e   un café . . . lait
f   une menthe . . . eau
g   un kir . . . crème de mûre

5 MIXED UP!

Put this jumbled dialogue between the waiter and yourself in the right order.

a   Qu'est-ce que vous avez choisi comme vin, madame?
b   Le menu à quatre-vingts, s'il vous plaît.
c   Un rosé d'Anjou, s'il vous plaît.
d   Et désirez-vous prendre un café?
e   Un steak au poivre . . . saignant.
f   Vous avez choisi un dessert, madame?
g   Et ensuite?
h   Non, merci. Ça va.
i   Bien, madame. Que prenez-vous comme entrée?
j   Oui, une pêche melba.
k   Un melon au porto, s'il vous plaît.
l   Avez-vous choisi, madame?

6 MIX AND MATCH

1	verte	a	Anjou
2	blanc	b	bouteille
3	saignant	c	kir
4	royal	d	salade
5	grande	e	steak

WORTH KNOWING

In restaurants, you'll often find two or three set meals with *un menu gastronomique* (generally the top-priced set meal with specialties of the region) and perhaps *un menu pour enfants* (special set meal for children). You'll also see displayed *le plat du jour* (the dish of the day). Some set meals will include the wine: *une carafe* or *un pichet* (pitcher) *de vin de pays* (local wine).

You'll find a wide range of eating places. If you'd like a quick meal, try *la brasserie, le snack-bar, le drugstore* or *le fast-food*. For something different, go to *crêperie* where you'll be able to taste delicious *galettes* (savory pancakes) and *crêpes* (pancakes) with all sorts of fillings. Try *une galette au jambon et fromage* (with ham and cheese) *une galette aux champignons* (with mushrooms) or *une crêpe à la confiture d'abricot* (with apricot jam).

Here's a selection of some of the most common snacks:

le croque-monsieur		toasted sandwich with ham and cheese
le croque-madame		toasted sandwich with ham and cheese and an egg on top
le sandwich	*au jambon*	ham sandwich
	au fromage	cheese sandwich
	au pâté	pâté sandwich
	aux rillettes	potted pork sandwich
	au saucisson	garlic sausage sandwich
le beignet		doughnut
le chausson aux pommes		apple turnover

This is a typical set meal:

Restaurant L'Escargot

Menu à 134,00 F

ENTRÉE AU CHOIX:	CHOICE OF APPETIZER:
terrine de pâté de canard	duck pâté terrine
ou	or
melon au porto	melon with port
ou	or
assiette de crudités	salad
PLAT PRINCIPAL AU CHOIX:	CHOICE OF MAIN DISH:
entrecôte grillée	grilled steak
ou	or
filet de porc normande	loin of pork Normandy
FROMAGE	CHEESE
DESSERTS	DESSERTS
Service 15% compris	*15% service included*

Finally, a few words on wine: You'll have heard of *vin blanc, vin rouge, vin rosé,* but have you heard of *vin jaune* and *vin de paille* (where the grapes are dried on straw before being pressed) from the Jura area? They're well worth tasting when you're next in that part of France. Wines vary from one region to another, from the fruity wines of Alsace to the dry white wines of the Loire valley. The wines of France fall into several categories:

● *vin ordinaire* is ordinary table wine.

- *vin de pays* has a higher ranking, in that it qualifies for departmental or local status, for example *vin de l'Ardèche*.
- *vins délimités de qualité supérieure* or *VDQS* are wines which are subject to regulations regarding the type of grapes used and the vinification.
- *Appellation d'origine contrôlée (AOC)* is the label under which the best wines are to be found.

To choose a good bottle of wine you need to look carefully both at the label, and the year the wine was produced (known as the *millésime*).

6 DOWN TO BUSINESS

KEY WORDS AND PHRASES

je suis Monsieur Pierre Bouillon	I'm Mr. Pierre Bouillon
Puis-je vous présenter mon collègue?	May I introduce my colleague to you?
j'ai rendez-vous avec Monsieur Doreau	I've an appointment with Monsieur Doreau
Quand pouvons-nous nous revoir?	When can we meet again?
Vous êtes libre lundi?	Are you free on Monday?
à quinze heures	at 3:00 p.m.
je crois qu'il est disponible	I think he's available
ah non, je regrette	oh no, I'm sorry
je voudrais parler à Monsieur Doreau	I'd like to speak to Monsieur Doreau
je rappellerai à partir de dix-sept heures	I'll call again after 5:00 p.m.
Quel est votre nom?	What's your name
Comment s'appellent-ils?	What are their names?
Vous habitez à Angers?	Do you live in Angers?
Vous êtes marié(e)?	Are you married?
Vous avez des enfants?	Do you have children?
Quel âge ont-ils?	How old are they?

ARRIVING FOR AN APPOINTMENT

M. BOUILLON	Bonjour, madame.
MME CELESTE	Bonjour, monsieur.
M. BOUILLON	Je suis Monsieur Pierre Bouillon de la société Cointreau. J'ai rendez-vous avec Monsieur Doreau à dix heures.
MME CELESTE	Oui. Asseyez-vous. Je vais le prévenir.
M. BOUILLON	Merci.
MME CELESTE	*(Going into Monsieur Doreau's office)* Monsieur Doreau, Monsieur Bouillon de la société Cointreau est arrivé.

MAY I INTRODUCE

M. BOUILLON	Puis-je vous présenter mon collègue, Monsieur Michaud.
M. DOREAU	Avec plaisir. Bonjour, Monsieur Michaud. Comment allez-vous?
M. MICHAUD	Bonjour, Monsieur Doreau. Très bien, merci.

ON THE TELEPHONE

MME CELESTE	Allô.
M. MICHAUD	Allô. Bonjour, madame. Je voudrais parler à Monsieur Doreau, s'il vous plaît.
MME CELESTE	Oui, monsieur. Mais Monsieur Doreau est en conférence.
M. MICHAUD	Quand est-ce que je peux le joindre?
MME CELESTE	A partir de cinq heures ce soir, monsieur.
M. MICHAUD	Bien, merci. Je rappellerai à partir de cinq heures. Au revoir, madame.
MME CELESTE	Au revoir, monsieur.

ARRANGING ANOTHER MEETING

M. BOUILLON	Bien, Monsieur Michaud, quand pouvons-nous nous revoir?
M. MICHAUD	Eh bien, pourquoi pas mercredi, quatorze heures?
M. BOUILLON	Mercredi, quatorze heures . . . Non, ce n'est pas possible. Est-ce possible jeudi à quinze heures?
M. MICHAUD	Jeudi, quinze heures . . . tout a fait!
M. BOUILLON	D'accord. Très bien.

I'D LIKE TO MEET . . . , TOO

M. BOUILLON	Je voudrais aussi rencontrer Monsieur Larchet, jeudi après-midi.
M. MICHAUD	Jeudi après-midi. Oui, je crois qu'il est disponible.
M. BOUILLON	Très bien. C'est parfait.

ARRANGING TO MEET

M. JAMET	Est-ce que vous êtes libre lundi à quinze heures?
MLLE COCHIN	Ah non, je regrette, pas lundi à quinze heures.
M. JAMET	Et jeudi à dix-huit heures?
MLLE COCHIN	Dix-huit heures . . . c'est parfait, oui.
M. JAMET	Entendu. Au revoir, mademoiselle.
MLLE COCHIN	Au revoir, monsieur.

ARRIVING FOR AN APPOINTMENT

MARIE-PIERRE	Pardon, monsieur. Monsieur Michaud?
M. MICHAUD	Oui, tout à fait.
MARIE-PIERRE	Marie-Pierre Méchineau, bonjour.
M. MICHAUD	Ah, Marie-Pierre, bonjour. Nous avons rendez-vous, n'est-ce pas?
MARIE-PIERRE	Oui, à neuf heures.
M. MICHAUD	Bien. Entrez, s'il vous plaît.

HOW CAN I CONTACT YOU?

MARIE-PIERRE	Monsieur Michaud, vous pouvez me donner votre numéro de téléphone au bureau, s'il vous plaît?
M. MICHAUD	Oui. bien sûr. C'est le quarante et un.
MARIE-PIERRE	Oui.
M. MICHAUD	Trente-sept . . .
MARIE-PIERRE	Oui.
M. MICHAUD	Trente, zéro, zéro. Poste quarante-deux, quarante.
MARIE-PIERRE	D'accord, merci beaucoup. Et votre numéro de télex?
M. MICHAUD	Alors le télex, sept cent vingts, neuf cent quatre-vingt six.
MARIE-PIERRE	Bien. Vous avez un numéro de fax?
M. MICHAUD	Oui, bien sûr. C'est le quarante et un, quarante-trois, trente, quatorze.
MARIE-PIERRE	D'accord, merci beaucoup.

SOCIALIZING

MARIE-PIERRE	Quel est votre nom?
M. BOUILLON	Pierre Bouillon.
MARIE-PIERRE	Vous êtes d'Angers?
M. BOUILLON	Non, je ne suis pas d'Angers.
MARIE-PIERRE	Vous êtes d'où?
M. BOUILLON	Je suis de Tours.
MARIE-PIERRE	Mais vous habitez à Angers maintenant?
M. BOUILLON	Oui, bien sûr.
MARIE-PIERRE	Et vous aimez?
M. BOUILLON	Oui, tout à fait.

ASKING ABOUT SOMEONE'S FAMILY

MARIE-PIERRE	Quel est votre nom?
MME LEBRETON	Marie-Noël Lebreton.
MARIE-PIERRE	Vous êtes mariée?
MME LEBRETON	Oui, je suis mariée.
MARIE-PIERRE	Et vous avez des enfants?
MME LEBRETON	Oui, j'en ai trois.
MARIE-PIERRE	Quel âge ont-ils?
MME LEBRETON	Dix ans, huit ans et quatre ans.
MARIE-PIERRE	Et comment s'appellent-ils?
MME LEBRETON	François, Marie et Alice.
MARIE-PIERRE	Oh, c'est joli!

WORD LIST

la société	company
asseyez-vous	sit down
je vais le prévenir	I'll let him know
. . . est arrivé	. . . has arrived
allô	hello (on the phone)
en conférence	in a meeting
Pourquoi pas?	Why not?
tout à fait	absolutely
aussi	also
rencontrer	meet
entendu!	fine!
après-midi	afternoon
nous avions	we had
numéro de télex/fax	telex/fax number
Vous aimez (Angers)?	Do you like (Angers)?
joli(e)	pretty

EXPLANATIONS

BUSINESS INTRODUCTIONS

To introduce yourself, and say which company you work for:
Je suis Pierre Bouillon, de la société Cointreau
Je m'appelle Marie-Noël Lebreton, de la société Thompson
Je suis John Bell de la société Turbo

To introduce someone else:
Puis-je vous présenter mon collègue, Monsieur Michaud
Voici Marie-Pierre

Puis-je . . . ? is the equivalent of 'may I . . . ?'

APPOINTMENTS

To say you have an appointment:
J'ai rendez-vous avec Monsieur Doreau à dix heures

To find out when someone is free/available:
Vous êtes libre lundi à quinze heures?
Vous êtes disponible jeudi à neuf heures?

You can also say:
Quand pouvons-nous nous revoir? When can we meet again?

ON THE TELEPHONE

I'd like/May I speak to . . . (*on the telephone*)
Je voudrais parler à Monsieur Doreau
Puis-je parler à Monsieur Michaud?

To find out when you can get in touch with someone:
Quand est-ce que je peux le joindre? (him)
Quand est-ce que je peux la contacter? (her)

To say when you'll call again:
Je rappellerai à partir de cinq heures

When you give a French telephone or fax number to someone you have to break the number into pairs:

C'est le quarante-et-un, trente-sept, trente, zéro, zéro

Notice that 00 is *zéro zéro* and that 07 is *zéro sept*.

TALKING ABOUT FAMILIES

If asked how many children you have, say, for example:

J'en ai trois

En means 'of them' in sentences like:

Vous aves des enfants?
  {
  Oui, j'en ai trois
  Oui, j'en ai un
  Non, je n'en ai pas
  }

It can also mean 'some' or 'any':

Vous avez du pain?   *Oui, j'en ai*

Vous voulez de l'eau   *Non, je n'en veux pas*

How old are they? What are their names?

Quel âge ont-ils?

Comment s'appellent-ils?

Instead of repeating the noun les enfants, Marie–Pierre used *ils* meaning 'they'.

If the noun is masculine, use *il*:

Je voudrais rencontrer Monsieur Larchet

Oui, je crois qu'il est disponible

If it's feminine, use *elle*:

Est-ce que Mademoiselle Cochin est libre?

Non elle est au téléphone

If 'they' refers to a plural feminine noun, use *elles*

J'ai deux filles (daughters); *elles s'appellent Maude et Gabrielle*

VERBS

When you're talking with other people, you'll obviously use you (*vous*) and I (*je*) a lot. Remember that in French the verb ending changes much more often than in English.

With *vous*, almost all verbs end with -*ez*:

Vous habitez à Angers? Do you live in Angers?
Vous avez des enfants? Do you have any children?
Vous voulez un apéritif? Would you like an aperitif?

But one very common exception:

Vous êtes d'Angers? Are you from Angers?

With *je*, the endings are more varied:

Je regrette I'm sorry (*formal*)
Je vous remercie Thank you (*formal*)
Je crois qu'il est disponible I think he's free
Je vous dois combien? How much do I owe you?
Je vais prendre le menu à soixante I'll have the set meal at 60,00 F
J'ai un rendez-vous avec I've a meeting with Monsieur
  Monsieur Doreau Doreau
Je suis de Tours I'm from Tours
Je peux vous payer? Can I pay you?

EXERCISES

1 BUSINESS INTRODUCTIONS

a Introduce yourself.
b Say you have an appointment at 10:30 a.m. with Monsieur Doreau
c Introduce your colleague, Madame Méchineau to Monsieur Doreau.
d You have to arrange another meeting with Monsieur Doreau. Ask him when he's free.
e When he suggests a time, say you're sorry, you're not available.

2   SOCIALIZING

How would each of the people below answer these questions?:

Quel est votre nom?   *Vous avez des enfants?*
Vous êtes d'où?   *Quel âge ont-ils?*
Vous êtes marié(e)?   *Comment s'appellent-ils?*

a   Peter Brown from London, married with two children, Mary (10) and Phillip (12)
b   Jane Roberts from New York, married with three children, Simon (16), James (19) and Sally (22)
c   Pierre Benoît from Reims, married with no children

3   NUMBERS

What are the following telephone and fax numbers in French?

a   tél 41 32 78 00

_____

b   fax 41 78 61 67

_____

c   tél 44 56 78 09

_____

d   fax 44 54 12 60

_____

e   tél 010 33 70 57 64 15

_____

f   fax 010 33 70 24 67 89

_____

4   ANSWERS USING '*EN*'

Answer these questions, using *en* in each answer:

a   Vous avez des enfants?   *Yes, three.*
b   Vous avez un rendez-vous ce soir?   *Yes, two.*
c   Combien de tranches de saucisson   *I'd like ten.*
        voulez-vous?
d   Vous avez une voiture?   *Yes, one.*
e   Vous avez des chambres de libre?   *No, I haven't.*

5 WHAT'S MISSING?

Fill in the blanks:

VOUS	Allô, Je . . . . Sophie Thireau de la . . . . Turbo. Je . . . . parler . . . . Monsieur Fichu, s'il vous plaît.
MME CELESTE	Je . . . . madame. Monsieur Fichu est absent.
VOUS	Quand puis-je le . . . . ?
MME CELESTE	Ce soir, ... de dix-neuf heures.
VOUS	D'accord. . . . . beaucoup. madame. Je . . . à dix-neuf heures.

WORTH KNOWING

The French telephone network is divided into *Paris* (and its suburbs) and *la province* (the rest of France). All subscribers have an eight-figure number. To make a telephone call within France, you have three possibilities:

- within Paris or la province, dial the eight-figure number only

- from Paris to la province, dial 16, wait for the tone *(la tonalité)*, then dial the eight-figure number

- from la province to Paris, dial 16, wait for the tone, then dial 1, followed by the eight-figure number

To telephone Canada or the United States from France, dial 19 and wait for the tone, then 1 followed by the area code and the number you want to contact.

Here are a few useful telephone expressions:

Qui est à l'appareil?	Who's speaking?
Monsieur Bouillon à l'appareil	Monsieur Bouillon speaking

Veuillez patienter	
Conservez	hold the line
Ne quittez pas	
Poste quarante-deux	Extension 42
Vous pouvez me passer Marie-Pierre?	Can you put me through to Marie-Pierre?

It may be useful to know what your job is in French, or to be able to say what sort of work you do. Here are a few tips to help:

le président directeur général chairman
la secrétaire de direction personal assistant
le/la comptable accountant
le chef du personnel personnel manager
le cadre executive
l'ingénieur (m) engineer
le directeur des ventes sales manager
le banquier banker
le chef du service export export manager
l'infirmière/infirmier female nurse/male nurse
le contremaître foreman
le boulanger/la boulangère baker
l'hôtesse de l'air (f) flight attendant

Je travaille dans l'industrie automobile
I work in the car industry
Je travaille à la Chambre de Commerce
I work at the Chamber of Commerce
Je travaille dans l'agro-alimentaire
I work in the food industry
Je travaille chez Cointreau
I work at Cointreau's
Je suis à la retraite/retraité
I'm retired

CAN YOU GET BY?

Try these questions when you've finished the course. The
answers are on pages 110–111.

1 MEETING PEOPLE AND ORDERING DRINKS

a How do you greet people in the evening?

b How do you say: 'How are you?'

c How do you say: 'Where are you from?'

d Say 'please' and 'thank you' (give two answers).

e Say to the waiter: 'For me, an orange juice'.

2 SHOPPING

a Ask the shopkeeper: 'Do you have any apples?'

b Say you'd like three kilos of oranges.

c Ask how much it is.

d Tell the service station attendant: 'Fill it up with unleaded
super'.

e Ask for 12 stamps at the post office.

3 GETTING AROUND

a Say: 'First street on the right, second on the left, and then
straight ahead'.

b Ask: 'Is there a gas station nearby?'

c Stop a passer-by and ask what the time is.

d Say: 'I'd like a round-trip ticket to Bordeaux'.

e Somebody is speaking too fast. Say: 'I'm sorry but I don't
understand. Slowly, please'.

4 FINDING SOMEWHERE TO STAY

a Ask Monsieur Ocher whether there's a room available.
b Say you have a reservation for three nights, from June 3 till June 6.
c Say you'd like a room with a double bed and shower.
d Ask what time breakfast is served.
e Ask for your key at the hotel reception desk (key number is 215).

5 EATING OUT

a Tell Monsieur Veger you'd like two set meals at 97,00 F and one at 125,00 F.
b Ask for a bottle of white wine and a bottle of mineral water.
c At the pâtisserie, say you'd like a pastry with chocolate in the middle and a lemon tea.
d Ask for two black coffees and one with cream.
e Say: 'I'd like the bill, please'.

6 DOWN TO BUSINESS

a Introduce yourself: name, age, marital status, number of children.
b Ask Monsieur Doreau whether he's free on Thursday.
c Say you've an appointment with Monsieur Doreau at 4:00 p.m.
d Ask Monsieur Doreau whether he has a fax number.
e His number is 45 31 92 11. What does he tell you?

REFERENCE SECTION

PRONUNCIATION GUIDE

Coping with the sounds of a foreign language seems daunting at first. With time and practice, however, you'll soon manage to make yourself understood quite easily. Just listen carefully to what is being said and don't be disheartened if you cannot always make yourself understood first time. This is only a rough guide to pronunciation, but it will help you cope.

VOWELS

a1   brief as in 'apple' or 'lack'
     addition, salade

a2   prolonged as in 'car'
     âge, pâtisserie

e1   is generally similar to 'a' as in 'about'
     le, de, petit

e2   is similar to 'e' as in 'let'
     merci, essence, escargot
     at the end of words like *douche, grande, petite, e* is not
     pronounced
     in words ending in *-er* and *ez*, for example *aller, prenez,*
     it's pronounced like *é*

é   is similar to a shortened 'ay' as in 'day'
     marié, entrée

è/ê   is similar to *e2*
    collègue, crème, vous êtes
i   is similar to 'i' in police
    kilo, frites, tant pis
o   can be short as in 'odd'
    société, cognac
o   at the end of a word, or *ô*, is long, similar to 'o' as in
    'post'
    numéro, hôtel
oi   is pronounced 'wa'
    droite, bonsoir
ou   is pronounced 'oo'
    vous, bonjour
u   is similar to 'ew' as in 'threw'
    rue, super, une

NASALS

These are vowel sounds followed by an 'n'. Listen carefully to the examples on the casette.

1 *-in*   *vin*
   -un   *un steak, un plan de la ville*
   -ain   *pain*
   -ien   *bien, combien*
   -ein   *le plein*
2 *-en*   *entrez*
   -an   *blanc*
3 *-on*   *bon*

CONSONANTS

A consonant at the end of a word is often not pronounced: *vous voulez, petit, grand, anglais*. But there are some exceptions, for example, *cognac*.

The following consonants sound much the same in French and in English:

b; d; f; k; l; m; n; p; s; t; v; z

The following are slightly different:

c	+ *a, o, u* or a consonant is like 'c' in 'cot' *café, cointreau*
c	+ *e* or *i* is like 's' in 'signal' *celui-ci, merci, Béatrice*
ç	is like 's' in 'signal' *ça va, française*
ch	is like 'sh' in 'ship' *château, marché*
g	+ *a, o, u* or a consonant is like 'g' as in 'gap' *gauche, baguette, grand*
gn	is like 'n' in 'onion' *champagne*
h	is usually not pronounced *hôtel, heure*
j	is like 's' in 'pleasure' *je, Anjou*
ph	is like the English 'f' *pharmacie*
qu	is like 'k' in 'kilo' *quatre, quelle heure*
r	comes from the back of the mouth. Listen carefully to the examples on the tape *bière, restaurant, kir royal*
t	followed by *-ion* is pronounced 's' *station d'essence, réservation*
th	is like 't' in 'table' *thé*

NUMBERS

0	*zéro*	21	*vingt et un*
1	*un/une*	22	*vingt-deux*
2	*deux*	23	*vingt-trois*
3	*trois*	30	*trente*
4	*quatre*	40	*quarante*
5	*cinq*	50	*cinquante*
6	*six*	60	*soixante*
7	*sept*	70	*soixante-dix*
8	*huit*	71	*soixante et onze*
9	*neuf*	72	*soixante-douze*
10	*dix*	80	*quatre-vingts*
11	*onze*	81	*quatre-vingt-un*
12	*douze*	90	*quatre-vingt-dix*
13	*treize*	91	*quatre-vingt-onze*
14	*quatorze*	100	*cent*
15	*quinze*	101	*cent un*
16	*seize*	102	*cent deux*
17	*dix-sept*	200	*deux cents*
18	*dix-huit*	201	*deux cent un*
19	*dix-neuf*	300	*trois cents*
20	*vingt*	1000	*mille*

FIRST, SECOND, THIRD

1st	*premier/première*
2nd	*deuxième*
3rd	*troisième*
9th	*neuvième*
11th	*onzième*
21st	*vingt et unième*

DAYS OF THE WEEK

lundi	Monday	*vendredi*	Friday
mardi	Tuesday	*samedi*	Saturday
mercredi	Wednesday	*dimanche*	Sunday
jeudi	Thursday		

MONTHS OF THE YEAR

janvier	January	*juillet*	July
février	February	*août*	August
mars	March	*septembre*	September
avril	April	*octobre*	October
mai	May	*novembre*	November
juin	June	*décembre*	December

TEMPERATURE CONVERSIONS
. . . .

To change Fahrenheit to Centigrade, subtract 32 and multiply
by ⅚.

To change Centigrade to Fahrenheit, multiply by ⅚ and add 32.

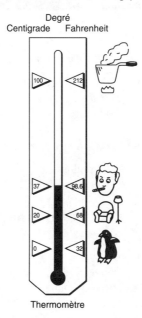

Degré
Centigrade   Fahrenheit

Thermomètre

WEIGHTS AND MEASURES

CENTIMETERS / INCHES
. . . .

It is usually unnecessary to make exact conversions from your
customary inches to the metric system used in France, but to give
you an approximate idea of how they compare, we give you the
following guide.

To convert **centimètres** into inches, multiply by .39.

To convert inches into **centimètres,** multiply by 2.54.

Centimètres

Pouces

METERS / FEET

1 meter **(mètre)** = 39.37 inches **(pouces)** 1 foot = 0.3 meters
= 3.28 feet   1 yard = 0.9 meters
= 1.09 yards

KILOGRAMS / POUNDS

1 kilogram **(kilo)** = 2.2 pounds
1 pound   = 0.45 kilogram

LITERS / QUARTS

1 liter = 1.06 quarts
4 liters = 1.06 gallons

For quick approximate conversion, multiply the number of gallons by 4 to get liters **(litres).** Divide the number of liters by 4 to get gallons.

Gasoline is sold by the liter in Europe; distance is measured in kilometers; and tire pressure is calculated in kilograms per square centimeter.

The following tables may help you.

LIQUID MEASURES
(APPROXIMATE)

LITERS	U.S. GALLONS	IMPERIAL GALLONS
30	8	6½
40	10½	8¾
50	13½	11
60	15½	13
70	18½	15½
80	21	17½

DISTANCE MEASURES
(APPROXIMATE)

KILOMETERS	MILES
1	.75
5	3
10	6
20	12
50	31
100	62

TIRE PRESSURE

LB./SQ. IN	KG./CM.^{2}
17	1.2
18	1.3
20	1.4
21	1.5
23	1.6
24	1.7
26	1.8
27	1.9
28	2.0
30	2.1
31	2.2
33	2.3
34	2.4
36	2.5
37	2.6
38	2.7
40	2.8

CONVERSION TABLES FOR CLOTHING SIZES

WOMEN

Shoes

American	4	5	5½	6	6½	7	7½	8	8½	9	9½	10
Continental	35	36	36	37	37	38	38	39	39	40	40	41

Dresses, suits

American	8	10	12	14	16	18
Continental	36	38	40	42	44	46

Blouses, sweaters

American	32	34	36	38	40	42
Continental	40	42	44	46	48	50

MEN

Shoes

American	7	7½	8	8½	9	9½	10	10½	11	11½
Continental	39	40	41	42	43	43	44	44	45	45

Suits, coats

American	34	36	38	40	42	44	46	48
Continental	44	46	48	50	52	54	56	58

Shirts

American	14	14½	15	15½	16	16½	17	17½
Continental	36	37	38	39	40	41	42	43

ROAD SIGNS

One-way street

DEVIATION

Detour

Danger ahead

Guarded railroad crossing

Yield

Stop

Right of way

Dangerous intersection ahead

Gasoline (petrol) ahead

Parking

Parking

No vehicles allowed

Dangerous curve

Pedestrian crossing

Oncoming traffic has right of way

No bicycles allowed

No parking allowed

No entry

No left turn

No U-turn

No passing

Border crossing

Traffic signal ahead

Speed limit

Traffic circle (roundabout) ahead

Minimum speed limit

All traffic turns left

End of no passing zone

Entrance to expressway

Expressway ends

OTHER ROAD SIGNS

Accotement non stabilisé	Soft shoulder
Allumez vos phares	Put on headlights
Arrêt interdit	No stopping
Attention	Caution
Céder le passage	Yield
Chaussée déformée	Poor roadway
Chute de pierres	Falling rocks
Circulation interdite	No thoroughfare
Descente (Pente) dangereuse	Steep slope (hill)
Déviation	Detour
Douane	Customs
École	School
Entrée interdite	No entrance
Fin d'interdiction de ____	End of ____ zone
Interdiction de doubler	No Passing
Interdiction de stationner	No Parking
Interdit aux piétons	No Pedestrians
Piste réservée aux transports publics	Lane for Public Transportation
Ralentir (Ralentissez)	Slow
Réservé aux piétons	Pedestrians only
Sens interdit	Wrong Way
Sens unique	One Way
Serrez à gauche (à droite)	Keep left (right)
Sortie d'autoroute	Freeway (throughway) Exit
Sortie de véhicules	Vehicle Exit
Stationnement autorisé	Parking Permitted
Stationnement interdit	No Parking
Tenez la droite (gauche)	Keep to the right (left)

Verglas		Icy Road
Virage dangereux		Dangerous Curve
Voie de dégagement		Private Entrance
Zone Bleue		Blue Zone (parking)

OTHER IMPORTANT SIGNS

À louer	*ah loo-ay*	For rent, hire
Ascenseur	*ah-sah<u>n</u>-ssuhr**	Elevator
Attention	*ah-tah<u>n</u>-ssyoh<u>n</u>*	Careful
À vendre	*ah vah<u>n</u>-druh*	For sale
Dames	*dahm*	Ladies
Danger	*dah<u>n</u>-zhay*	Danger
Danger de mort	*dah<u>n</u>-zhay duh mohr*	Danger of death
Défense de	*day-fah<u>n</u>ss duh*	Do not ____
Défense d'entrer	*day-fah<u>n</u>ss dah<u>n</u>-tray*	Do not enter
Défense de cracher	*day-fah<u>n</u>ss duh krah-shay*	No spitting
Défense de fumer	*day-fah<u>n</u>ss duh few-may*	No smoking
Défense de marcher sur l'herbe	*day-fah<u>n</u>ss duh marh-shay sewr lehrb*	Keep off the grass
Eau non potable	*oh noh<u>n</u> poh-tah-bluh*	Don't drink the water
École	*ay-kohl*	School
Entrée	*ah<u>n</u>-tray*	Entrance
Entrée interdite	*ah<u>n</u>-tray a<u>n</u>-tehr-deet*	No Entrance
Entrée libre	*ah<u>n</u>-tray lee-bruh*	Free Admission
Fermé	*fehr-may*	Closed
Fumeurs	*few-muhr*	Smokers
Hommes	*ohm*	Men
Hôpital	*oh-pee-tahl*	Hospital

* <u>n</u> indicates nasal pronunciation

Horaire	*oh-rehr*	Schedule
Libre	*lee-bruh*	Free, Unoccupied
Messieurs	*meh-ssyuh*	Gentlemen
Ne pas toucher	*nuh pah too-shay*	Don't touch
Non fumeurs	*nohn few-muhr*	Non smokers
Occupé	*oh-kew-pay*	Occupied
Ouvert	*oo-vehr*	Open
Passage souterrain	*pah-ssahzh soo-teh-ran*	Underground passage
Poussez	*poo-ssay*	Push
Privé	*pree-vay*	Private
Quai/Vole	*kay/vwah*	Track, Platform
Renseignements	*rahn-sseh-nyuh-mahn*	Information
Réservé	*ray-zehr-vay*	Reserved
Salle d'attente	*sahl dah-tahnt*	Waiting room
Soldes	*sohld*	Sales
Sonnez	*soh-nay*	Ring
Sortie	*sohr-tee*	Exit
Sortie de secours	*sohr-tee duh suh-koor*	Emergency exit
Stationnement interdit	*stah-ssyohn-mahn an-tehr-dee*	No parking
Tirez	*tee-ray*	Pull
Toilettes	*twah-leht*	Toilets

MENU ITEMS

APPETIZERS

Artichauts à la vinaigrette   artichokes in a vinaigrette dressing.

Cruditées variées   assorted vegetables—sliced tomatoes, shredded carrots, sliced cooked beets—in a vinaigrette dressing.

Escargots à la bourguignonne   snails cooked and served in the shell, seasoned with a garlic, shallot, and parsley butter.

Foie gras   fresh, often uncooked liver of a force-fed goose; sliced and served with toasted French bread slices.

Pâté   any of a number of meat loaves, made from puréed liver and usually also with meat—pork, veal, or chicken. **Pâté de foie gras** is made with goose liver; pâté de campagne is "of the country" and is a coarser mixed meat pâté; **pâté en croute** is a liver pâté encased in pastry.

Quiche lorraine   an egg custard tart, sometimes with bacon strips or bits; some versions now also made with Gruyère cheese.

Quenelles   light dumplings, usually made from **brochet** (pike) but also from shellfish; served in a white sauce.

Rillettes   a pork mixture that has been potted, then served as a spread, usually with French bread.

Terrine   A type of pâté, usually served from a deep pot rather than sliced as pâté would be. Terrines can be made from pork, poultry, game, or fish.

SOUPS

Some of those that appear on menus are the following:

Bisque d'écrevisses   a creamy soup made with crawfish; other bisques are made with lobster, shrimp, or oysters.

Bouillabaisse   a seafood stew, made with a variety of fish and shellfish depending on the region, seasoned with saffron and fennel or pernod.

Consommé   a clear broth, made usually from chicken or beef and flavored with herbs; **en gelée** is consommé that has been jelled and sliced; **madrilène** is with tomatoes; **printanier** has a variety of vegetables.

Crème   A creamy soup, made from any number of vegetables and usually enriched with egg yolks. **D'Argenteuil** is cream of asparagus soup; **de volaille** is a creamy chicken soup.

Petite marmite   a rich consommé served with the meat and vegetables.

Potage   a coarser soup, usually made with a purée of vegetables; some varieties of potage are **parmentier** (leeks and potatoes), **au cresson** (watercress), **julienne** (shredded vegetables).

Soupe à l'oignon   famous French onion soup, served over French bread and covered with cheese.

Velouté   a creamy soup, most common of which is **de volaille** (cream of chicken) and **de tomate** (tomato).

EGG DISHES

As is true for most of the continent, eggs are not eaten for breakfast but rather are served as a beginning course in a variety of preparations.

Oeufs bercy   eggs baked with sausages in a tomato sauce.

Oeufs en cocotte   eggs gently baked in individual cups until softly cooked, sometimes with cream, then eaten with a spoon.

Oeufs en geleé   poached eggs that are set into jelled consommé and served chilled as a salad.

Omelette   a French omelette is puffy and contains a variety of fillings—**aux fines herbes** is with a mixture of parsley, chives, and tarragon.

Piperade   scrambled eggs mixed with tomatoes, onions, and sweet peppers.

Soufflé   soufflés can be made with almost any ingredients— vegetables, chicken livers, cheese, ham, and so on; they are always light and puffy.

POULTRY AND GAME

la caille	*lah kahy*	quail
le cerf	*luh sehr*	venison
la canard, caneton	*luh kah-nahr, kahn-tohn*	duckling
le chapon	*luh shah-pohn*	capon
le chevreuil	*luh shuh-vruhy*	venison
le cochon de lait	*luh koh-shohn duh leh*	suckling pig
la dinde	*lah dand*	turkey
le faisan	*luh feh-zahn*	pheasant
le lapin	*luh lah-pan*	rabbit
le lièvre	*luh lyeh-vruh*	hare
l'oie *(f.)*	*lwah*	goose
le perdreau, la perdrix	*luh pehr-droh, lah pehr-dree*	partridge
le pigeon, le pigeonneau	*luh pee-zhohn, luh pee-zhoh-noh*	squab
la pintade, le pintadeau	*lah pan-tahd, luh pan-tah-doh*	guinea fowl
la poule	*lah pool*	stewing fowl
le poulet, poussin, la volaille	*luh poo-leh, poo-ssan, lah voh-lahy*	chicken

Suprême de volaille is the fillet from a young chicken breast, usually served with a sauce or garnish.

FISH

les anchois	*lay zahn-shwah*	anchovies
les anguilles	*lay zahn-gee*	eel
le bar	*luh bahr*	bass (hake)
la barbue	*lah bahr-bew*	brill
la baudroie	*lah boh-drwah*	anglerfish, monkfish
le brochet	*luh broh-sheh*	pike
le cabillaud	*luh kah-bee-yoh*	cod
le calmar	*luh kahl-mahr*	squid
la carpe	*lah kahrp*	carp
le carrelet	*luh kahr-leh*	flounder
le congre	*luh kohn-gruh*	conger eel
les crevettes	*lay kruh-veht*	shrimp
la daurade	*lah doh-rahd*	porgy
les écrevisses	*lay zay-kruh-veess*	crawfish
les escargots	*lay zehss-kahr-goh*	snails
les harengs (fumés)	*lay ah-rahn (few-may)*	herring (smoked)
le homard	*luh oh-mahr*	lobster
les huîtres	*lay zwee-truh*	oysters
la lamproie	*lah lahn-prwah*	lamprey
la langouste	*lah lahn-goosst*	spiny lobster
les langoustines	*lay lahn-goo-ssteen*	large shrimp
la lotte	*lah loht*	monkfish
le loup de mer	*luh loo duh mehr*	sea bass
le maquereau	*luh mah-kroh*	mackerel
le merlan	*luh mehr-lahn*	whiting

la morue	*lah moh-rew*	cod
les moules	*lay mool*	mussels
les palourdes	*lay pah-loord*	clams
la perche	*lah pehrsh*	perch
les poulpes	*lay poolp*	octopus
la rascasse	*lah rahss-kahss*	scorpionfish
les sardines	*lay sahr-deen*	sardines
le saumon	*luh soh-mohn*	salmon
les scampi	*lay skahn-pee*	large shrimp
le thon	*luh tohn*	tuna
la truite	*lah trweet*	trout
le turbot	*luh tewr-boh*	European turbot

MEAT

l'agneau *(m.)*	*lah-nyoh*	lamb
le bœuf	*luh buhf*	beef
la chèvre	*lah sheh-vruh*	goat
le jambon	*luh zhahn-bohn*	ham
le mouton	*luh moo-tohn*	mutton
le porc	*luh pohr*	pork
le veau	*luh voh*	veal
les andouilles	*lay zahn-dooy*	pork sausages
le bifteck	*luh beef-tehk*	steak
le boudin	*luh boo-dan*	blood sausage
le carré d'agneau	*luh kah-ray dah-hyoh*	rack of lamb
le cervelas	*luh sehr-vuh-lah*	garlicky pork sausage
la cervelle	*lah sehr-vehl*	brains
la charcuterie	*lah shahr-kew-tree*	assorted sausages, pâtés, and terrines

le chateaubriand	*luh shah-toh-bree-ah<u>n</u>*	porterhouse steak
la côte de bœuf	*lah koht duh buhf*	ribs of beef
les côtelettes	*lay koht-leht*	cutlets
les côtes de porc, de veau	*lay koht duh pohr, duh voh*	chops, pork or veal
les crépinettes	*lay kray-pee-neht*	small sausages
l'entrecôte *(f.)*	*lah<u>n</u>-truh-koht*	sirloin steak
l'escalope *(f.)*	*lehss-kah-lohp*	cutlet
le filet de bœuf	*luh fee-leh-duh buhf*	fillet of beef
le foie	*luh fwah*	liver
le gigot d'agneau	*luh zhee-goh dah-nyoh*	leg of lamb
la langue	*lah lah<u>n</u>g*	tongue
le lard	*luh lahr*	bacon
les médaillons de veau	*lay may-dah-yoh<u>n</u> duh voh*	small rounds of veal
les noisettes	*lay nwah-zeht*	small fillets
les pieds de porc	*lay pyay duh pohr*	pig's feet
le ris de veau	*luh ree duh voh*	veal sweetbreads
les rognons d'agneau	*lay roh-nyoh<u>n</u> dah-nyoh*	lamb kidneys
le rosbif	*luh rohss-beef*	roast beef
les saucisses	*lay soh-sseess*	sausages
la selle d'agneau	*lah sehl dah-nyoh*	saddle of lamb
le steak	*luh stehk*	steak
le tournedos	*luh toor-nuh-doh*	small fillets of beef
les tripes	*lay treep*	tripe
Is it ____?	**C'est ____?**	*seh*
baked	**au four**	*oh foor*
boiled	**bouilli(e)**	*boo-yee*

braised (stewed)	**braisé(e)**	*breh-zey*
broiled (grilled)	**grillé(e)**	*gree-yay*
roasted	**rôti(e)**	*roh-tee*
poached	**poché(e)**	*poh-shay*
I like the steak _____.	**Je préfère le steak _____.**	*zhuh pray-fehr luh stehk*
well–done	**bien cuit(e)**	*byan kwee*
medium	**à point**	*ah pwan*
rare	**saignant(e)**	*seh-hyahn*
tender	**tendre**	*tahn-druh*

PREPARATIONS AND SAUCES

Of necessity, these descriptions are very brief and generalized, but they should give you an impression of what to expect.

aioli   mayonnaise heavily flavored with garlic

allemande   a light (blond) sauce

à la bonne femme   white wine sauce with vegetables

alsacienne   with sauerkraut

béarnaise   a butter-egg sauce flavored with shallots, wine, and tarragon

bercy   basic meat or fish sauce

beurre blanc   butter sauce flavored with shallots and wine

beurre noir   browned butter sauce

blanquette   an egg-enriched cream sauce, usually part of a stewed dish

bordelaise   a dish prepared with Bordeaux wine

bourguignonne   a dish prepared with Burgundy red wine

bretonne   a dish that includes beans

caen   a dish made with Calvados (apple brandy)

chantilly   a sauce of whipped cream and hollandaise; or as a dessert, sweetened whipped cream

chasseur   a sauce made with mushrooms, white wine, shallots, and parsley

choron   a béarnaise sauce with tomatoes

coquilles   a preparation served in a scallop shell

coulibiac   a preparation served in a pastry shell

crécy   a dish made with carrots

daube   a stew, usually beef, made with red wine, onions, and garlic

demi-deuil   when slices of truffles are inserted beneath the skin of a chicken

diable   a spice sauce, usually with chili or cayenne pepper

duxelles   a mushroom mixture, usually as a stuffing or sauce base

estragon   a dish made with tarragon

farcie   a stuffing, or forcemeat filling

fenouil   a sauce made with fennel

financière   madeira sauce with truffles

fines herbes   a dish made with a variety of chopped fresh herbs

florentine   a dish that includes spinach

forestière   a dish made with wild mushrooms

fricassée   a stewed or potted dish, usually chicken

gratin   a crusty baked dish, named for the dish in which it is cooked

hollandaise   an egg yolk and butter sauce, with vinegar or lemon juice

jardinière   a dish with fresh vegetables

lyonnaise   a preparation made with onions

madère   a dish made with madeira wine

maître d'hôtel   a butter sauce with parsley and lemon juice

marchand de vin   a sauce with a meat stock and red wine

meunière   a simple dish lightly dusted with flour and sauteed, served in a lemon-butter sauce

mornay   a simple white sauce with grated cheese, usually gruyère

mousseline   a hollandaise sauce with whipped cream

moutarde   with mustard

nantua   a basic white sauce with cream and shellfish

normande   either a fish sauce with oysters or shrimp; or a sauce with apples

parmentier   a dish with potatoes

périgourdine   with truffles

poivrade   a dark sauce, seasoned with pepper

provençale   a vegetable garnish, usually with tomatoes, olives, anchovies, and garlic

quenelles   light-as-air dumplings made from fish or shellfish

ragoût   a thick stew

rémoulade   a mayonnaise flavored with mustard and sometimes capers

véronique   a dish with grapes

verte   a green mayonnaise, flavored with parsley and other herbs

vinaigrette   an oil and vinegar dressing for salads

vol-au-vent   a puff-pastry shell in which is usually served a creamed meat dish

VEGETABLES

l'artichaut *(m.)*	*lahr-tee-shoh*	artichoke
les asperges	*lay zahss-pehrzh*	asparagus

l'aubergine *(f.)*	*loh-behr-zheen*	eggplant
la betterave	*lah beh-trahv*	beet
les carottes	*lay cah-roht*	carrots
le céleri	*luh sayl-ree*	celery
le céleri rave	*luh sahl-ree-rahv*	knob celery
les champignons	*lay shah<u>n</u>-pee-nyoh<u>n</u>*	mushrooms
le chou	*luh shoo*	cabbage (green)
le chou-fleur	*luh shoo-fluhr*	cauliflower
la courgette	*lah koor-zheht*	zucchini
le cresson	*luh kreh-ssoh<u>n</u>*	watercress
les épinards	*lay zay-pee-nahr*	spinach
les flageolets	*lay flah-zhoh-leh*	green shell beans
les haricots verts	*lay ah-ree-koh vehr*	green beans
les oignons	*lay zoh-nyoh<u>n</u>*	onions
l'oseille *(f.)*	*loh-zehy*	sorrel
le piment	*luh pee-mah<u>n</u>*	green pepper
les pois	*lay pwah*	peas
le poireau	*luh pwah-roh*	leek
les pommes de terre	*lay pohm duh tehr*	potatoes
la tomate	*lah toh-maht*	tomato

CHEESE COURSE

The cheese course is offered after the meat course and before the dessert.

What is that cheese?	**Quel est ce fromage?**	*kehl eh suh froh-mahzh*
Is it ____?	**Est–il ____?**	*eh-teel*
mild	**maigre**	*meh-gruh*
sharp	**piquant**	*pee-kah<u>n</u>*

| hard | **fermenté** | *fehr-mahn-tay* |
| soft | **à pâte molle** | *ah paht mohl* |

Among the more popular cheeses are the following.

Banon   Made from sheep's or goat's milk, a soft cheese with a natural rind; a mild cheese with a mild nutty flavor.

Bleu d'auvergne   Made from cow's milk, this soft cheese has an internal mold and when cut, the veins are visible. With a very sharp flavor.

Boursin   A soft cow's milk cheese, with a mild flavor, sometimes enhanced with herbs.

Brie   A variety of cheeses made from cow's milk and with a bloomy rind. Varieties range in flavor from mild to very pronounced, some with a fruity flavor.

Camembert   Less delicate than brie, but also a cow's milk cheese with a bloomy rind. Should be eaten firm.

Cantal   A cow's milk cheese that varies with length of aging. Some varieties are softer and milder, while more aged ones are hard and with a more pronounced flavor.

Chèvre   Any of an almost infinite variety of goat's milk cheeses, which vary from very soft to quite firm, and from mild and creamy to tart and crumbly. There will always be a few chèvres on the cheese tray.

Colombière   This cow's milk cheese is soft and supple, with a mild flavor.

Munster   A cow's milk cheese that is soft and spicy, with a tangy flavor. In Alsace, where the cheese comes from, it is eaten young.

Pont-l'évêque   A cow's milk cheese that is very smooth and supple, with a pronounced flavor.

Port-salut   The brand name for the Saint-Paulin from the monastery of Port-du-Salut.

Reblochon   A soft cow's milk cheese with a mild and creamy flavor.

Roquefort   A sheep's milk cheese that is soft and pungent. The cheese is cured in caves, an ancient process with rigid standards for production. Texture is very buttery.

Saint-paulin   Made from cow's milk, this is a velvety smooth cheese with a mild flavor.

Tomme de savoie   A mild cow's milk cheese with a nutty flavor.

Petit Suisse is a fresh, unsalted cheese made from cow's milk and enriched with cream, then molded into heart shapes and sprinkled with sugar; it is a common dessert.

Fromage à la crème is *fromage blanc,* a rich, creamy white cheese made from unskimmed cow's milk. It is eaten topped with cream and sugar for breakfast.

Fondue is a specialty of Switzerland and parts of France that border on Switzerland. It is a large pot of bubbling melted cheese (usually gruyère or emmenthal), into which is dipped cubes of French bread. Fondue is served as a warming lunch or dinner course.

Raciette is a specialty of French-speaking Switzerland. It involves the slow melting of a hard cheese, usually alongside a roaring fire, during which the diners scrape off the cheese as it melts onto slices of French bread.

FRUITS AND NUTS

l'abricot	*lah-bree-koh*	apricot
l'ananas	*lah-nah-nah*	pineapple
la banane	*lah bah-nahn*	banana
les cassis	*lay kah-sseess*	black currants
la cerise	*lah suh-reez*	cherry
le citron	*luh see-troh<u>n</u>*	lemon

la datte	*lah daht*	date
la figue	*lah feeg*	fig
les fraises	*lay frehz*	strawberries
les fraises des bois	*lay frehz duh bwah*	wild strawberries
les framboises	*lay frah<u>n</u>-bwahz*	raspberries
les groseilles	*lay groh-sehy*	red currants
la limette	*lah lee-meht*	lime
la mandarine	*lah mah<u>n</u>-dah-reen*	tangerine
le melon	*luh muh-loh<u>n</u>*	melon
les mûres	*lay mewr*	mulberries
les myrtilles	*lay meer-tee*	blueberries
l'orange	*loh-rah<u>n</u>zh*	orange
la noix de coco	*lah nwah duh koh-koh*	coconut
le pample-mousse	*luh pah<u>n</u>-pluh-mooss*	grapefruit
la pêche	*lah pehsh*	peach
la poire	*lah pwahr*	pear
la pomme	*lah pohm*	apple
la prune	*lah prewn*	plum
le pruneau	*luh prew-noh*	prune
le raisin	*luh reh-za<u>n</u>*	grape
l'amande *(f.)*	*lah-mah<u>n</u>d*	almond
le marron	*luh mah-roh<u>n</u>*	chestnut
la noisette	*lah nwah-zeht*	hazelnut
les noix	*lay nwah*	nuts

SWEET DESSERTS

Bararoise A bavarian cream; mont-blanc is a bavarian cream made with chestnuts.

Beignets Fritters, often made from fruit such as apple.

Bombe An ice cream construction, often with different flavors and sometimes also with sherbet.

Charlotte   An assemblage of sponge fingers and pudding; usually the sponge cake is used to line the dish and pudding is in the center.

Crème caramel   An egg custard served with a caramel sauce.

Crêpes   Dessert crêpes, the most famous of which are **Crêpes Suzette,** made with orange flavoring and served flaming with Grand Marnier.

Gâteau   An elaborate layer cake, made with thin layers of sponge cake and pastry cream, and decorated.

Mousse au chocolat   An airy pudding made with chocolate cream, eggs, and brandy, garnished with whipped cream.

Macédoine de fruits   A fresh fruit salad.

Oeufs à la neige   Soft meringue ovals served floating on a custard sauce.

Omelette Norvégienne   Baked Alaska.

Pâtisserie   Pastry selection of any variety, including éclairs, millefeuilles, savarin, Saint-Honoré (cream puff cake).

Poires Hélène   A poached pear, served with vanilla ice cream and chocolate sauce.

Profiteroles   Cream puffs, served with chocolate sauce.

Soufflé   An endless variety of sweet soufflés, the famous one being the Grand Marnier soufflé.

Tarte   Open-faced fruit pies, often made with apples or plums.

In addition, ice cream is a French favorite, as is sherbet and granité (fruit ice). Here's how to ask for these:

ice cream	**une glace**	*ewn glahss*
chocolate	**au chocolat**	*oh shoh-koh-lah*
vanilla	**à la vanille**	*ah lah vah-nee*
strawberry	**aux fraises**	*oh frehz*
sundae	**une coupe**	*ewn koop*
sherbet	**un sorbet**	*uhn sohr-beh*
fruit ice	**un granité**	*uhn grah-nee-tay*

KEY TO THE EXERCISES

1 SAYING HELLO AND ORDERING DRINKS

1 GREETINGS

a Bonjour, Marie-Pierre. Comment allez-vous?/
(Comment) ça va?
b Bonsoir, Anne.
c Bonjour, Monsieur Bouillon. Comment allez-vous?
d Au revoir Monsieur Doreau.
e Bonjour, madame.

2 AT THE 'CAFE'

S'il vous plaît
Deux bières, s'il vous plaît
Pression, s'il vous plaît

3 NUMBERS

a trois ● cinq ● sept ● huit ● dix
b dix ● cinq ● six ● neuf ● dix

4 ORDERING DRINKS

a Un thé au citron, s'il vous plaît.
b Deux cafés, s'il vous plaît.
c Trois jus d'orange, s'il vous plaît.
d Un cointreau, s'il vous plaît.

5 MIX AND MATCH

1c ● 2d ● 3b ● 4e ● 5a

2 SHOPPING

1 HERE'S YOUR SHOPPING LIST

J'aimerais . . . *or* Je voudrais . . . s'il vous plaît.

a une bouteille de vin rouge
b trois baguettes
c quatre cent cinquante grammes de gruyère
d huit tranches de saucisson (à l'ail)
e deux kilos de pommes
f une livre de tomates

2 MIXED UP

b ● a ● e ● d ● c

– Qu'est-ce que vous voulez?
– 450 grammes de gruyère, s'il vous plaît.
– Et avec ceci?
– Du saucisson.
– Combien de tranches?
– Huit tranches de saucisson.
– Vous voulez autre chose?
– Des pommes.
– Combien de kilos?
– Deux kilos de pommes.

3 HOW MUCH?

a 25,60 F ● b 2,80 F ● c 14,33 F ● d quinze francs ●
e neuf francs cinquante ● f treize francs vingt-neuf

4 AT THE FRUIT MARKET

– Bonjour, mademoiselle.
– Un kilo de pommes.
– Six tomates, s'il vous plaît.
– Merci. C'est combien les oranges?

5   A FEW NECESSITIES

a Je voudrais un guide d'Angers, s'il vous plaît.
b Je voudrais changer deux cents livres sterling en francs français.
c Je voudrais quatre timbres pour la Grande-Bretagne.
d Je voudrais vingt litres d'essence sans plomb.

3   TRAVELING AROUND

1   DIRECTIONS

a Vous prenez la Rue Toussaint. Vous continuez tout droit et le château est devant vous.
b Vous prenez/montez (*go up*) le Boulevard du Roi René sur votre gauche et vous allez jusqu'aux feux (*traffic lights*). Puis vous tournez à gauche. Vous prenez le Boulevard du Maréchal Foch. Vous continuez tout droit et le Jardin du Mail est sur votre droite.
c Vous prenez/descendez (*go down*) la Rue St Aubin. Au bout de la Rue St Aubin, vous tournez à gauche. Puis vous prenez la Rue Toussaint. Vous continuez tout droit. Le musée est sur votre gauche.

2   WHAT TIME IS IT?

a dix heures vingt-cinq (du matin)
b une heure quarante (de l'après-midi) or treize heures quarante
c quatre heures cinq (du matin)
d neuf heures trente (du soir) or vingt et une heures trente
e quinze heures dix
f treize heures quinze
g vingt et une heures trente-cinq
h zéro heure quarante-deux

3 HOW DO I GET TO …?

- Excusez-moi/Pardon.
- Pour aller au château, s'il vous plaît?
- Pardon. Plus lentement, s'il vous plaît.
- A gauche . . . le boulevard du Roi René.
- D'accord. Et c'est loin?
- D'accord/Bien. Merci beaucoup/Je vous remercie beaucoup.
- Au revoir.

4 BUYING TRAIN TICKETS

a Un aller-retour pour Lyon, en seconde.
b Deux allers simples pour Lille, en première.
c Un aller simple pour Marseille, en seconde.
d Il y a un train pour Saumur à dix heures?
e C'est quel quai?
f C'est combien un aller-retour en première?

5 OPENING AND CLOSING TIMES

a The museum is open from 10:00 until 17:30 every day except Sunday when it is closed.
b The castle is open from 9:30 until 18:00; closed on Mondays.
c The cathedral is open between 9:00 and 18:00 every day.

4 FINDING SOMEWHERE TO STAY

1 RESERVING HOTEL ROOMS

a Vous avez deux chambres avec/à un grand lit, avec bain, pour trois nuits?
b Vous avez une chambre à deux lits, avec douche, pour cette nuit?
c Je voudrais réserver une chambre à un lit, avec cabinet de toilette, du 9 au 12 août.

d Je voudrais réserver une chambre à un grand lit et un lit
   d'enfant, avec douche, pour la semaine prochaine.
e Vous avez une chambre avec douche pour un enfant et une
   chambre avec bain pour deux adultes?

2 MIX AND MATCH

1c ● 2d ● 3a ● 4b

3 SPEAKING TO THE RECEPTIONIST

a Vous avez des chambres de libre, s'il vous plaît?
b C'est combien la chambre avec cabinet de toilette?
c (Est-ce que) le petit déjeuner est compris?
d A quelle heure est-ce que vous servez le petit déjeuner?

4 THERE MUST BE SOME MISTAKE!

– Bonsoir.
– J'ai une réservation pour une chambre à un grand lit, avec
  douche.
– Je m'appelle Stuart.
– Je ne comprends pas.
– (Est-ce qu')il y a un autre hôtel près d'ici?
– Merci.

5 FILL IN THE BLANKS

Nom: Paine
Prénom: Liz
Numéro du passeport: 934507 D
Numéro d'immatriculation du véhicule: H 789 ABC
Nombre de personnes: adultes: deux
                                  enfants: trois

Caravane: oui
Tente: oui
Electricité: oui
Nombre de nuits: sept
Dates: du vingt-trois au vingt-neuf juillet

5 EATING OUT

1 WHICH WOULD YOU CHOOSE?

1c ● 2a ● 3c ● 4c ● 5a

2 WHAT DID THEY ORDER?

Apéritif Marie-Pierre: un kir royal ● Pierrick: un whisky
● Marc: un ricard
Entrée Marie-Pierre, Pierrick et Marc: les escargots
Plat principal Pierrick et Marc: un filet mignon ●
Marie-Pierre: une sole meunière
Vins avec les escargots, un Anjou blanc, puis un Chinon
Dessert Marie-Pierre et Marc: une Fôret-Noire au
chocolat ● Pierrick: une pêche melba
Café Marie-Pierre et Marc: un café
Digestif Pierrick: un petit cognac ● Marc: un cointreau

3 IN A RESTAURANT

a   Une table pour trois, s'il vous plaît.
b   Un menu à soixante-quinze (francs) et deux à cent
    quarante (francs).
c   Un martini, un whisky et un kir pour moi.
d   Un steak saignant et un steak à point *or* Deux steaks, un
    saignant et l'autre à point, et une sole meunière.
e   Une bouteille d'Anjou blanc.
f   Trois pêches melba.
g   Deux cafés et un crème.
h   L'addition s'il vous plaît.

4 FILL THE GAPS

a au   b à la   c au   d à la   e au   f à l'   g à la

5 MIXED UP!

l ● b ● i ● k ● g ● e ● a ● c ● f ● j ● d ● h

6 MIX AND MATCH

1d ● 2a ● 3e ● 4c ● 5b

6 MEETING PEOPLE AND DOING BUSINESS

BUSINESS INTRODUCTIONS

a Je m'appelle or je suis Madame/Mademoiselle/
Monsieur . . .
b J'ai un rendez-vous à dix heures trente avec Monsieur
Doreau.
c Voici ma collègue Madame Méchineau.
d Quand est-ce que vous êtes libre?/Quand êtes-vous libre?/
Vous êtes libre quand?
e Je suis désolé. Je ne suis pas libre.

2 SOCIALIZING

a Je m'appelle Peter Brown. Je suis de Londres. Je suis marié
et j'ai deux enfants, Mary dix ans et Philip douze ans.
b Je m'appelle Jane Roberts. Je suis de New York. Je suis
mariée et j'ai trois enfants, Simon seize ans, James dix-
neuf ans et Sally vingt-deux ans.
c Je m'appelle Pierre Benoît. Je suis de Reims. Je suis marié
mais je n'ai pas d'enfants.

3 NUMBERS

a quarante et un; trente-deux; soixante-dix-huit; zéro zéro
b quarante et un; soixante-dix-huit; soixante et un; soixante-
sept
c quarante-quatre; cinquante-six; soixante-dix-huit; zéro
neuf
d quarante-quatre; cinquante-quatre; douze; soixante
e zéro dix; trente-trois; soixante-dix; cinquante-sept;
soixante-quatre; quinze
f zéro dix; trente-trois; soixante-dix; vingt-quatre; soixante-
sept; quatre-vingt-neuf

4   ANSWERS USING 'EN'

a   J'en ai trois.
b   J'en ai deux.
c   J'en voudrais dix.
d   J'en ai une.
e   Je n'en ai pas.

5   WHAT'S MISSING?

VOUS	m'appelle ● société ● voudrais ● à
MME CELESTE	suis désolée
VOUS	contacter
MME CELESTE	à partir de
VOUS	merci ● rappellerai

CAN YOU GET BY?

1   MEETING PEOPLE AND ORDERING DRINKS

a   Bonsoir, madame/mademoiselle/monsieur.
b   Comment allez-vous?/Ça va?
c   Vous êtes d'où?
d   S'il vous plaît ● Merci/Je vous remercie.
e   Pour moi, un jus d'orange.

2   SHOPPING

a   Vous avez des pommes?
b   Je voudrais trois kilos d'oranges.
c   C'est combien?
d   Le plein de super sans plomb.
e   Je voudrais douze timbres pour la Grande-Bretagne.

3   OUT AND AROUND

a   La première rue à droite, la deuxième à gauche et (c'est) tout droit.

b Il y a une station d'essence/une station-service près d'ici?

c Excusez-moi madame/monsieur. Quelle heure est-il/il est?

d Je voudrais un aller-retour pour Bordeaux.

e Je suis désolé, mais je ne comprends pas. Lentement, s'il vous plaît.

4 FINDING SOMEWHERE TO STAY

a Vous avez des chambres de libre?

b J'ai une réservation pour trois nuits (à partir) du 3 (jusqu') au 6 juin.

c J'aimerais une chambre à un grand lit, avec douche.

d Vous servez le petit déjeuner à quelle heure?/à quelle heure est-ce que vous servez le petit déjeuner?

e Je voudrais la clef numéro deux cent quinze.

5 EATING OUT

a Deux menus à quatre-vingt-dix-sept et un à cent vingt-cinq.

b (J'aimerais) une bouteille de vin blanc et une bouteille d'eau minérale.

c J'aimerais/Je voudrais un pain au chocolat et un thé au citron.

d Deux cafés et un crème, s'il vous plaît.

e L'addition, s'il vous plaît.

6 DOWN TO BUSINESS

a Je m'appelle . . . . J'ai . . . ans. Je suis marié(e)/Je ne suis pas marié(e)/Je suis célibataire (*single*). J'ai . . . enfants/Je n'ai pas d'enfants.

b Vous êtes libre jeudi?

c J'ai un rendez-vous avec Monsieur Doreau à quatre heures de l'après-midi/seize heures.

d Vous avez un numéro de fax?

e Le quarante-cinq   trente et un   quatre-vingt douze onze.

WORD LISTS

FRENCH-ENGLISH

A

d'accord fine/OK
l'addition (f) bill
l'adulte (m/f) adult
l'agneau (m) lamb
vous aimez . . . ? do you like . . . ?
aller to go
allez! go on!
l'aller-retour (m) round-trip
l'aller simple (m) one way
l'allumette (f) match
alors then
Américain(e) American
l'Amérique (f) America
anglais(e) English
je m'appelle my name is
l'après-midi (m/f) afternoon
l'arrivée arrival
vous arrivez you arrive
l'asperge (f) asparagus
asseyez-vous sit down
au revoir goodbye
autre chose (f) something else
nous avions we had

B

les bagages (m) luggage
la baguette French stick
le bain bath
la banque bank
le beurre butter
la bière beer
bien sûr of course
blanc white
boire to drink
la boîte box
bonjour (m) good morning
bonsoir (m) good evening/good night
la boulangerie baker's
la bouteille bottle
au bureau at the office/at work
le bureau de tabac tobacconist's

C

ça va? how are you?

ça va I'm fine

ça ne fait rien it does not matter

le cabinet de toilette washroom

le café coffee

le car bus

la caravane mobile home

la carotte carrot

la carte postale postcard

la cathédrale cathedral

ceci this

avec ceci with this

cela that

cela vous fait . . . that will be . . .

celui-ci this one

celui-là that one

le centre-ville town centre

la cerise cherry

certainement certainly

la chambre room

changer to change

le château castle

chaud(e) hot/ warm

le chocolat chocolate

vous avez choisi? have you chosen?

le cinquante et un aniseed based aperitif

le citron lemon

le citron pressé squeezed lemon juice

la clef key

le/la collègue colleague

combien how much/many

c'est combien? how much is it?

je vous dois combien? how much do I owe you?

comme as

comment how

comment allez-vous? how are you?

comment s'appellent-ils? what are their names?

complet/complète full

comprise included

compter to count

le concombre cucumber

en conférence (f) in a meeting

la crème de cassis blackcurrant liqueur

la crème de mûre blackberry liqueur

la crème de pêche peach liqueur

je crois I believe
cru(e) cured, raw
cuit(e) cooked

D

dans in
le départ departure
derrière behind
vous désirez? would you like?
désolé(e) sorry
deuxième second
le digestif liqueur
disponible available
donner to give
la douche shower
la douzaine dozen
droite right

E

l'eau water
également also
l'électricité (f) electricity
l'emplacement (m) place (at campsite)
encore once again
les enfants (m) children
entendu! fine!
l'entrée (f) starter
entrez come in
environ about
envoyer to send
épais(se) thick
les épinards (m) spinach

les escargots (m) snails
l'étage floor
l'essence (f) gasoline/regular gas
vous êtes you are
excusez-moi excuse me
l'express (m) espresso (coffee)

F

facile easy
faire to do
fermer to close
le filet mignon beef fillet
fin(e) fine
les flageolets (m) dwarf kidney beans
la Fôret-Noire black forest cake
la fraise strawberry
français(e) French
froid(e) cold
le fromage cheese

G

la gare station
la gare routière bus station
gauche left
le guide guide
grand(e) big
la Grande-Bretagne Great Britain
gratuit(e) free

H

l'heure (f) time, hour
les haricots verts (m) green beans
l'horaire (m) timetable

I

ici here
il y a there is/are
inscrit booked

J

le jambon ham
joindre to get hold of
joli(e) pretty
le jus d'orange orange juice
jusqu'à till/up to

K

le kir white wine with blackcurrant liqueur
le kir royal champagne (or sparkling wine) with blackcurrant liqueur

L

là there
là-bas over there
le lait milk
les légumes (m) vegetables
lentement slowly
libre available/free

le lit bed
à un grand lit with a double bed
la livre 1 pound (½ kg.); a pound (sterling)
loin far

M

maintenant now
malheureusement unfortunately
le marché market
marié(e) married
le menu set meal
merci (beaucoup/bien) thank you (very much)
moi me
pour moi for me
moyen(ne) average
le musée museum

N

le nom name
la note bill
la nuit night
le numéro number

O

l'œuf (m) egg
où where
d'où from where
ouvert(e) open

P

le pain bread

le pain au chocolat pastry with chocolate in the middle

le pain aux raisins pastry with currants

pardon excuse me

parfait(e) perfect

le parfum flavor

le parking parking lot

partir to leave

le passeport passport

les pâtisseries (f) cakes and pastries

payer to pay

la pêche peach

la pêche melba peach melba

la personne person

petit(e) small

le petit déjeuner breakfast

je peux . . . ? can I . . . ?

la pharmacie drugstore

à pied on foot

la place space, square (in a town)

avec plaisir with pleasure

s'il vous plaît please

le plan map

le plat dish

le plein (d'essence) fill it up

à point medium (steak)

la pomme apple

la pomme de terre potato

les pommes frites (f) French fries

le porto port

le poste extension (telephone)

pourquoi why

premier/première first

première classe first class

prendre to take

vous prenez? are you taking?

préparer to prepare

près near

tout près d'ici very near here

la pression draft beer

prévenir to let somebody know

je vous en prie my pleasure

prochain(e) next

puis-je . . . ? may I . . . ?

Q

le quai platform
quand when
quel(le) what
quelle heure est-il?
what time is it?
*à quelle heure ferme
. . . ?* what time
does . . . close?
quel âge ont-ils?
how old are they?

R

je rappellerai I'll call
again
regarder to look
je regrette I'm sorry
je vous remercie thank
you
rencontrer to meet
le rendez-vous
appointment
réserver to book
revoir to meet
again
rien du tout
nothing at all
la rue street
la rue piétonne
pedestrian street

S

saignant(e) rare
(steak)
la salade verte lettuce
la salle de bains
bathroom
le saucisson (à l'ail)
(garlic) sausage
en seconde (classe) in
second class
la semaine week
ce sera tout that will be
all
je vous sers I'll serve you
vous servez you serve
la société company
le soir evening/night
ce soir tonight
la sole meunière sole
fried in butter with
lemon and parsley
nous sommes we are
la spécialité specialty
la station d'essence gas
station
je suis I am
vous suivez you follow
le super premium gas
le super sans plomb
premium unleaded
en supplément extra

T

tant pis   never mind

tchin   cheers

le *téléphérique*   cable car

la *tente*   tent

tenez   here you are

le *thé*   tea

le *thé nature*   plain tea

le *timbre*   stamps

la *tomate*   tomato

tous les jours   everyday

tout à fait   absolutely

tout de suite   right away

tout droit   straight ahead

la *tranche*   slice

vous *traversez*   you cross

très bien   very well

la *truite*   trout

V

vas-y   go on

la *viande*   meat

la *viennoiserie*   viennese pastry

la *ville*   town

le *vin*   wine

voici   here it is/you are

voilà   there it is/you are

la *voiture*   car

votre   your

à la *vôtre*   cheers

je *voudrais*   I'd like

vous *voulez . . . ?*   do you want . . . ?

voyons   let's see

ENGLISH-FRENCH

A

about environ
absolutely tout à fait
adult l'adulte (m/f)
afternoon l'après-midi (m/f)
again encore
also également
America l'Amérique (f)
American l'Americain(e)
anise-based aperitif le cinquante et un (lit. *fifty-one*)
apple la pomme
appointment le rendez-vous
arrive arriver; *you arrive* vous arrivez
arrival l'arrivée
as comme
asparagus l'asperge (f)
automobile/car la voiture
available disponible
available/free libre
average moyen(ne)

B

bakery la boulangerie
bank la banque
bath la bain
bathroom la salle de bains
be etre; *I am* je suis; *you are* vous êtes

bed le lit
beef filet le filet mignon
beer la bière; *draft beer* la pression
behind derrière
believe coire; *I believe* je crois
big grand(e)
bill (check) l'addition (f)
bill (currency) la note
black forest cake la Fôret-Noire
blackberry liqueur la crème de mûre
blackcurrant liqueur la crème de cassis
booked, fully inscrit
bottle la bouteille
box la boîte
bread le pain; *French bread* la baguette
breakfast le petit déjeuner
bus le car
bus station la gare routière
butter le beurre

C

cable car le téléphérique
cakes/pastries les pâtisseries (f); *black forest cake* la Foret-Noire
call appeller; *I'll call again* je rappellerai

can pouvoir; *I can* je peux; *may I . . . ?* puis-je . . . ?

car/automobile la voiture

carrot la carotte

castle le château

cathedral la cathédrale

certainly certainement

champagne with blackcurrant liqueur le kir royal

change changer

check/bill (restaurant) l'addition (f)

cheers à la vôtre, tchin

cheese le fromage

cherry la cerise

children les enfants (m)

chocolate le chocolat

choose choisir; *have you chosen?* vous avez choisi?

close fermer

coffee le café

cold froid(e)

colleague le/la collègue

come in entrez

company (business) la société

cooked cuit(e)

combine/get hold of joindre

count compter

cross traverser; *you cross* vous traversez

cucumber le concombre

cured, raw cru(e)

D

departure le départ

dish le plat

do faire

double bed, with à un grand lit

dozen la douzaine

draft beer la pression

drink boire

drugstore la pharmacie

E

easy facile

egg l'œuf (m)

electricity l'électricité (f)

English anglais(e)

espresso (coffee) l'express (m)

evening/night le soir; *good evening* bon soir (m)

everyday tous les jours

excuse me excusez-moi/pardon

extension (telephone) le poste

extra en supplément

F

far loin

fill it up (with gas) le plein (d'essence)

fine fin(e)

fine!/OK! d'accord!/entendu!!

first   premier/première
first class   première classe
first course   l'entrée (f)
flavor   le parfum
floor   l'étage
follow   suivre; *you follow*
   vous suivez
foot   le pied; *on foot*   à
   pied
for me   pour moi
free   gratuit(e)
French   français(e)
French bread   la baguette
French fries   les pommes frites
   (f)
from where   d'où
full   complet/complète

G

gas station   la station
   d'essence
gasoline/regular gas   l'essence
   (f); *premium gas*   le super;
   unleaded super   le super
   sans plomb
give   donner
go   aller
go on   vas-y; *go on!*   allez!
good   bon(ne); *good evening/*
   good night   bon soir (m);
   good morning   bonjour (m)
goodbye/good night   au revoir
Great Britain   la Grande-
   Bretagne

green beans   les haricots verts
   (m)
guide   le guide

H

ham   le jambon
he   il
here   ici; *here it is/you are*
   voici; *here you are*
   tenez
hot/warm   chaud(e)
how   comment; *how are you?*
   comment allez-vous?/ça
   va?
how much/many   combien;
   how much do I owe you?   je
   vous dois combien? *how*
   much is it?   c'est
   combien?
how old are they?   quel âge
   ont-ils?

I

I   je
in   dans
included   comprise

K

key   la clef
kidney beans (small)   les
   flageolets (m)

L

lamb l'agneau (m)
leave partir
left gauche
lemon le citron; *squeezed lemon juice* le citron pressé
lettuce la salade verte
like/want aimer/desirer/vouloir; *I'd like* je voudrais; *do you like . . . ?* vous aimez . . . ? *do you want . . . ?* vous voulez. . . ? *would you like?* vous désirez?
liqueur le digestif
look regarder
luggage les bagages (m)

M

map le plan
market le marché
married marié(e)
matter importer; *it does not matter* n'importe/ça ne fait rien
match l'allumette (f)
me moi; *for me* pour moi
meal le repas; *set meal* le menu
meat la viande
meet rencontrer; *meet again* revoir

meeting conférence; *in a meeting* en conférence (f)
medium (steak) à point
milk le lait
mobile home la caravane
morning le matin; *good morning* bonjour
museum le musée

N

name le nom; *my name is* je m'appelle *what are their names?* comment s'appellent-ils?
near près; *very near here* tout près d'ici
never mind tant pis
next prochain(e)
night la nuit; *good night* au revoir
nothing rien; *nothing at all* rien du tout
now maintenant
number le numéro
of course bien sûr

O

office le bureau; *at the office/at work* au bureau
one way (trip) l'aller simple (m)
open ouvert(e)
orange juice le jus d'orange
over there là-bas

P

parking garage/lot   le parking

pay   payer

passport   le passeport

pastry   la pâtisserie; *pastry with chocolate in the middle* le pain au chocolat; *pastry with currants* le pain aux raisins; *viennese pastry* la viennoiserie

peach   la pêche; *peach melba* la pêche melba; *peach liqueur* la crème de pêche

perfect   parfait(e)

person   la personne

place (at campsite) l'emplacement (m)

platform   le quai

please   s'il vous plaît

pleasure   plaisir; *with pleasure* avec plaisir

pork fillet   le filet mignon

port   le porto

postcard   la carte postale

pound (sterling)   la livre

pound (unit of weight)   un demi kilo

potato   la pomme de terre

precede/prevent/let somebody know   prévenir

pretty   joli(e)

prepare   préparer

R

rare (steak)   saignant(e)

raw   cru(e)

regret, grieve   regretter; *I'm sorry* je regrette

reserve/book   réserver

right   droite

right away   tout de suite

room   la chambre

round trip   l'aller'retour (m)

S

sausage   le saucisson; *garlic sausage* le saucisson à l'ail

second   deuxième

second class   seconde classe; *in second class* en seconde (classe)

see   voir; *let's see* voyons

send   envoyer

serve   servir; *I'll serve you* je vous sers; *you serve* vous servez

she   elle

shower   la douche

sit down   asseyez-vous

slice   la tranche

slowly   lentement

small   petit(e)

snails   les escargots (m)

sole (fried in butter with lemon and parsley)   la sole (meunière)

something else   autre chose (f)
sorry   désolé(e)
space/square (in a town)   la place
specialty   la spécialité
spinach   les épinards (m)
stamps   le timbre
steak   le bifteck; *medium (steak)* a point; *rare (steak)* saignant
station   la gare
straight ahead   tout droit
strawberry   la fraise
street   la rue; *pedestrian street* la rue piétonne

T

take   prendre; *are you taking?* vous prenez
tea   le thé; *plain tea* le thé nature
tent   la tente
thank you   je vous remercie; *thank you (very much)* merci (beaucoup/bien)
that   cela; *that will be . . .* cela vous fait . . . ; *that will be all* ce sera tout
that one   celui-là
then   alors
there   là
there is/are   il y a
there it is/there you are   voilà
they   ils (m)/elles (f)

thick   épais(se)
this   ceci; *with this* avec ceci
this one   celui-ci
time/hour   l'heure (f); *what time does . . . close?* à quelle heure ferme . . . ? *what time is it?* quelle heure est-il?
timetable   l'horaire (m)
tobacconist's   le bureau de tabac
tomato   la tomate
tonight   ce soir
town   la ville; *town center* le centre-ville
trout   la truite

U

unfortunately   malheureusement
until/up to   jusqu'à

V

vegetables   les légumes (m)
very well   très bien
viennese pastry   la viennoiserie

W

want/like   aimer/désirer/vouloir; *I'd like* je voudrais; *do you like . . . ?*

vous aimez . . . ? *do you want . . . ?* vous voulez . . . ? *would you like?* vous désirez?

washroom/dressing room la cabinet de toilette

water l'eau

we nous; *we are* nous sommes; *we had* nous avions

week la semaine

what quel(le); *what time does . . . close?* à quelle heure ferme . . . ? *what time is it?* quelle heur est-il?

when quand

where où

white blanc

white wine le vin blanc

white wine with blackcurrant liqueur le kir

why pourquoi

wine le vin

worse pis; *so much the worse/too bad/never mind* tant pis

Y

you vous (polite); tu (familiar)

you are vous êtes

you arrive vous arrivez

you cross vous traversez

you follow vous suivez

you serve vous servez

your votre

NOTES

N O T E S

N O T E S